TIBET

Patricia Levy

MARSHALL CAVENDISH
New York • London • Sydney

Reference edition reprinted 2000 by
Marshall Cavendish Corporation
99 White Plains Road
Tarrytown
New York 10591

© Times Media Private Limited 1996

Originated and designed by
Times Books International, an imprint of
Times Media Private Limited, a member of the
Times Publishing Group

Printed in Malaysia

Library of Congress Cataloging-in-Publication Data:
Levy, Patricia Marjorie, 1951-
    Tibet / Patricia Marjorie Levy.
        p.   cm.—(Cultures Of The World)
    Includes bibliographical references and index.
    Summary: Examines the lives and times of the Tibetan
people, their cultural complexities, the country's astonishing
geography, and its economic and political status.
        ISBN 0-7614-0277-2 (lib. bdg.)
    1. Tibet (China)—Juvenile literature. 2. Tibet
(China) I. Title. II. Series.
DS786.L456 1996
951'.5—dc20   95–42223
                      CIP
                      AC

INTRODUCTION

TIBET IS AN ANCIENT COUNTRY that has been a source of wonder and mystery to people all over the world for hundreds of years. Its recent history has been a tragic and turbulent one. A way of life that was static for centuries is gone, probably forever, as the once independent nation faces its 25th year as an autonomous region of China.

The Tibetan people have made their home in one of the most inhospitable, but also one of the most stunning, regions in the world. Tibet includes the highest point on earth, Mt. Everest, as well as vast areas of land too cold and windswept for any vegetation to grow. This book examines the lives of those hardy people, their ancient culture, the country's astonishing geography, and its economic and political realities today. It examines the religious beliefs that shape their lives and their struggle to maintain their traditional way of life.

CONTENTS

A Tibetan woman in traditional dress.

CONTENTS

A statue of the Buddha housed in the Jokhang Temple.

GEOGRAPHY

TIBET IS THE HIGHEST region in the world with an average altitude of 16,000 feet (4,875 meters). Isolated by vast mountain ranges that form its western, northern, and southern borders, it is one of the world's least populated areas. A large portion of the total land area of 474,008 square miles (1,228,000 square kilometers) is uninhabited, barren desert.

Tibet is a landlocked country, bounded on the west by India and on the south by Myanmar (Burma), India, Bhutan, and Nepal. On the east it borders the Chinese provinces of Sichuan and Yunnan, and in the north its neighbors are the autonomous province of Sinkiang and the province of Qinghai.

GEOGRAPHICAL REGIONS

THE NORTHERN PLATEAU The Northern Plateau, locally called the Chang Tang, is one of the most inhospitable places on the planet, with low temperatures, high winds, lack of rainfall, and sparse vegetation. It is the largest region of Tibet, covering about half of Tibet's surface area. The western border is created by the Karakoram Range, which includes K2, the second highest peak in the world. To the north lie the Kunlun Mountains. The plateau contains no major rivers and rainfall is sparse, but the lack of drainage on the mountainous plateau has caused salt lakes to develop. In the north of the plateau is the Zaidam, or salt marsh. This was once a huge lake but is gradually drying up. It provides a habitat for many rare marsh birds.

Few humans have ever set foot in most of this region. Some of the nomadic people of Tibet make use of the vast plains of the plateau, but they generally keep to the southern parts of the region where the land is more hospitable.

The Northern Plateau has an average elevation of 15,000 feet (4,570 meters). Most visitors to the area experience altitude sickness for the first few days.

Opposite: **The Xêgar Monastery. Tibet's terrain is so rugged that many communities must be built into the sides of mountains.**

The fertile soil of the Outer Plateau allows farmers in the town of Xêgar to rely exclusively on agriculture.

THE OUTER PLATEAU This is a great arc of land extending 2,200 miles (3,500 kilometers) west to east in a relatively thin band south of the Northern Plateau. It is bordered to the west by the Karakoram Range and to the south by the Himalaya. Through the center runs the great Yarlung Zangbo River. In the west, the soil is poor and rainfall is low, making agriculture very difficult, but farther east in the arc, many of the valleys support a flourishing agriculture. This is because of warmer temperatures, adequate rainfall, and a large supply of river water to irrigate the land.

The majority of Tibet's small population lives in the Outer Plateau and most of its cities and towns are located there, including Lhasa, the capital city.

THE SOUTHEASTERN PLATEAU The arc of the Outer Plateau gradually falls in altitude until it reaches the Southeastern Plateau. Here the vegetation is very different and includes dense forests and subtropical plants. The soft sedimentary rocks that characterize this region are gouged into vast ravines and gorges by the huge and powerful rivers that originate in Tibet and then nourish the countries to the south. The southeastern region is itself closed off by the north-south mountain ranges of this area. Between them flow the Yangtze, Mekong, and Salween rivers. These great rivers of the East flow north to south, almost parallel to one another, with only the mountain ranges separating them. Eventually they emerge in the Chinese provinces of Sichuan and Yunnan.

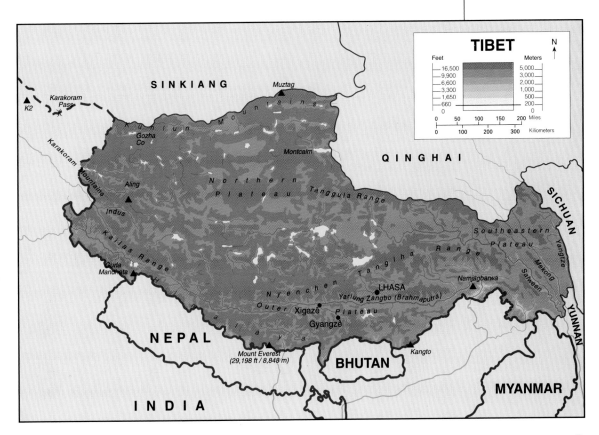

Mountain rivers carve paths through the rock of the Himalaya.

MOUNTAINS

Himalaya is a Sanskrit word meaning abode of snow. The Himalaya is an enormous chain of mountains that extends from Pakistan eastwards across Kashmir, northern India, the southern borders of Tibet, and finally into Nepal, Sikkim, and Bhutan. The Tethys and the Great Himalaya, which form Tibet's southern border, are the two sections of this range in Tibet.

Mount Everest, which lies on the border between Tibet and Nepal, is just one of the vast mountains that form the Great Himalaya. Other well known Himalayan peaks are Namjagbarwa at 25,445 feet (7,756 meters) and Gurla Mandhata at 25,355 feet (7,728 meters).

In the west of Tibet lies the Karakoram Range, which stretches all the way into Pakistan. The Nan Shan rise to a height of 25,340 feet (7,724 meters), dominating the northeast horizon. Extending 1,500 miles (2,410 kilometers), they create a natural border between the Northern Plateau and Sinkiang autonomous region of China.

MOUNT EVEREST

Qomolangma ("cho-mo-LUNG-ma"), or "goddess mother of the world," as the Tibetans call Mount Everest, is the highest point on earth at 29,198 feet (8,848 meters) above sea level. Named after Sir George Everest, a surveyor general of India who first recorded the location and height of the mountain, it lies on the border between Tibet and Nepal.

Attempts to climb the mountain began in 1920 with the opening of the Tibetan route. However, the high altitudes, wind, and cold air caused the failure and death of many who dared to try.

Tibetan monks were reluctant to allow climbers to use the Tibetan route, fearful that the gods of the mountain would kill them. Paintings remaining in now deserted monasteries show the fate they believed would befall anyone who set foot on the mountain.

When China closed its doors to the outside world in 1951, routes through Nepal were sought. In 1953, Edmund Hillary of New Zealand and Sherpa Tenzing Norgay of Nepal reached the summit from the southeast ridge. After that, many more followed until today there is a waiting list several years long of groups who wish to attempt to reach the top. But only a limited number of teams can make the ascent each year because the climbing season is so short and there are very few safe locations for base camps.

Sherpas are a tribe of mountain people particularly skilled at mountain climbing, and especially sought after by Everest expeditions. Sherpa Sungdare holds the world record, having made the ascent four times.

The temperatures on Mount Everest are so low that nothing decays. As a result the mountain is littered with garbage from climbing expeditions.

WATERWAYS

Many of Asia's most important rivers have their source in the Tibetan highlands, the high plateau of Tibet, and neighboring Qinghai province. The Indus, which flows northwest across Tibet and into India, forms in western Tibet from the glacial streams of the Himalaya. The Salween forms the border between Myanmar and Thailand before reaching the sea 1,750 miles (2,815 kilometers) from its source in central Tibet.

The Mekong travels southeast for 2,600 miles (4,200 kilometers) from its source north of Tibet and eventually empties into the South China Sea. The Yangtze forms huge gorges in southeastern Tibet before traveling south into Yunnan province. The Huang He, the Yellow River, rises in the southeast and flows east through China where, 2,900 miles (4,667 kilometers) from its source, it empties into the Gulf of Zhili.

Most of Tibet's rivers originate in lakes formed by glacial debris. But on the Northern Plateau, where rainfall is sparse, lake water evaporates very quickly, leaving behind valuable salt deposits. Lake Nam Co, which lies 1,500 feet (4,591 meters) above sea level, is one example of this.

GLACIERS

A glacier is produced from the repeated melting and evaporation of snow. The fluffy snow that falls in the Tibetan mountains is transformed by repeated evaporation into hard granules, which are covered each year by new fallen snow, burying them deeper and deeper. The weight of the overlying snow then causes the granules to melt and recrystallize, until there are no air pockets left, eventually creating a solid mass of ice, or a glacier.

Once the glacier reaches a depth of about 200 feet (65 meters) the lower layers of packed ice become liquid and begin to flow, allowing the glacier to move. The movement erodes mountains, forming sharp, jagged edges and peaks. Glaciers are the source of the majority of the major rivers that originate in Tibet.

THE YARLUNG ZANGBO RIVER This is Tibet's major waterway. As it travels east towards the Southeastern Plateau it winds through sandbanks, splitting and reforming again until it reaches the Namjagbarwa, a mountain in the east of Tibet, where it makes a sharp horseshoe turn and runs south into Bangladesh as the Brahmaputra. In the eastern Himalayas, the river falls 11,000 feet (3,350 meters). Explorers once hoped that the sharp drop in altitude was the result of an enormous waterfall, but in 1924 the river was completely mapped and no fall of over 30 feet (9 meters) was recorded. In fact, the river falls through a series of rapids where the water travels at about 33 feet (10 meters) per second.

A stretch of the Yarlung Zangbo between Lhasa and Gyangzê.

CLIMATE

Tibet's weather patterns are influenced by its position north of the Himalaya. From June to September, the summer monsoons sweep across the Indian subcontinent. The rains produce lush vegetation on the southern slopes of the Himalaya, but the northern slopes remain bare and rocky since the mountains are so high that most of the rain never reaches the northern side.

A beautiful display of the lush vegetation that develops on the southern slopes of the Himalaya.

Tibet has a temperate climate with spring beginning in March or April. By midsummer the rainy season has begun, but rainfall is intermittent in the south and the east, and rare in the west and the north. Average rainfall in Tibet is only 15 inches (38.1 cm) per year—very low for a country that is dependent on agriculture—so the monsoons are welcomed by the farmers. On the Northern Plateau, where temperatures are very low and winds very high, the lack of rain frequently causes dust storms.

By September temperatures drop again, signaling the coming of autumn. Dramatic changes in the weather are not uncommon in summer and autumn when the temperature can drop from as high as 100°F (37.4°C) in the day to below freezing at night.

In December the weather turns very cold. On the Northern Plateau, temperatures drop as low as -40°F (-39°C). Winters are cold and dry but very sunny.

FLORA AND FAUNA

Weather conditions and high altitudes make it very difficult for any but the hardiest of plants and animals to survive. At the very highest points, permanent snow and ice prevent anything from growing. But just below the snowline, alpine flowers, such as gentians and rock jasmine, flourish. Only plants that can retain moisture and protect themselves from the winds generally survive, so lichens, which are low-lying and grow inside moisture-retaining cushions, form the basic pioneer plants in these regions. Animals that are typical at these heights are the snow leopard, an endangered species, brown bears, and snow grouse. Birds such as geese, snow pigeons, and griffon vultures also inhabit these regions.

On the Northern Plateau, where grasses dominate the landscape, a different kind of life exists. Wader birds spend the summer months in the salt marshes of the far north. On the higher slopes, the alpine plants reappear. Other animals found in this region are wild yaks, feral sheep and goats, wolves, foxes, snow leopards, and the Tibetan antelope, distinguished by its vertical antlers, which grow up to 28 inches (70 centimeters) long.

In the southeast of the country several species of trees develop. At these lower altitudes, Tibetan fir, mountain ash, laurel, bamboo, magnolia, and oak are sheltered from the wind and grow to usual heights, unlike the dwarfed trees of the north. Tigers, musk deer, squirrels, macaques, and black bears inhabit these forests.

Frost touches the petals of these red flowers growing wild outside Nyalam.

CITIES AND TOWNS

With a population of approximately 10,000, Gyangzê qualifies as one of the largest towns in Tibet. Gyangzê relies primarily on agriculture, although many of its people are also engaged in handicrafts.

The total population of Tibet, which is roughly the size of western Europe, is only 2,280,000. The majority of the population inhabit the Outer Plateau, living in the capital, Lhasa, or other small towns that dot the area.

Lhasa is situated in central southern Tibet on a tributary of the Yarlung Zangbo River, the Lhasa He. The city stands about 12,070 feet (3,660 meters) above sea level and is surrounded by mountains. It is linked to other provinces of China by modern highways. There are regular flights

from the airport outside the capital to Chengdu and Qinghai in China.

With a population of 60,000 and a history that dates back 1,400 years, modern Lhasa has become two cities in one—a modern Chinese business area and the traditional city that still stands the way it has for centuries. The ancient city revolves around the market where traders from all over Tibet meet to barter their newly acquired goods. Unpaved roads that bend and twist are lined with whitewashed houses that slope inwards, allowing residents to look out over the crowds of people.

In sharp contrast, the newer part of the city has wide, straight, paved streets lined with planted trees. The modern buildings house government departments, hotels, offices, and apartments. The majority of the Chinese who live in Tibet make Lhasa their home.

The second largest town, with a population of 40,000, is Xigazê, standing at an altitude of 12,800 feet (3,900 meters). It is situated at the confluence of the Yarlung Zangbo and Nu Jiang rivers in the midst of a rich farming area. The town was once dominated by a monastery, but now a modern Chinese area stands at the center of the town. About 50 miles (80 kilometers) southeast of Xigazê lies the town of Gyangzê. These two towns are connected by a modern road and are very similar in character.

Zhanang is located southeast of Lhasa and like other Tibetan towns has a new Chinese-built section surrounding the older heart of the city. Its population together with the adjacent town of Nêdong is 25,000. The town is famous for its pears and apples, which come from the surrounding orchards.

A street in the modern section of Lhasa.

Each year, the town of Gyangzê hosts a horseback riding competition. People from all over Tibet come to watch and take part in this grand spectacle of horsemanship.

17

HISTORY

TIBET HAS BEEN CLOSED to most of the world, including archaeologists, for most of its modern history. Because of this, very little is known of the prehistory of Tibet, except that a civilization existed there for thousands of years. There is some evidence of a Stone Age culture in Tibet. Recent excavations in Tingri, near the border with Nepal, have revealed evidence of an indigenous Stone Age culture.

Legends tell of a man called Nyatri Tsenpo whose origins are thought to be Indian. He is said to have appeared on a mountain in the Yarlung Valley in central-southern Tibet where he was adopted as chieftain by the local people. This story can be traced back to as early as 500 B.C.

The 26 kings who succeeded Nyatri Tsenpo were animists practicing a religion called Bön. In the fourth century A.D., during the reign of the 28th king, legend says that Buddhist scriptures fell from the sky into the king's palace. The following century was dominated by the conflict between the two religions.

SONGSTEN GAMPO (557–649)

Songsten Gampo is the first king whose reign historians can date. Tibet's first great historical leader, he became the 33rd king at the age of 13. Prior to his rule, Tibet, divided by warring tribes, had been virtually ignored by its powerful neighbors, India, Nepal, and China. Under Songsten Gampo, Tibet became a powerful military and cultural force. In a series of military campaigns and treaties with local chieftains, he took control of a region extending from China in the east to Turkey in the west and India in the south.

By 648, Songsten had invaded northern India and was continuing to expand his empire, threatening China's western border. Rather than oppose him, his neighbors chose to form alliances through marriage, and

Above: **The ancient flag of Tibet is still flown over many refugee settlements in India and elsewhere. The sun rising behind a snowy mountain surrounded by 12 blue and red rays represents the legendary ancestors of Tibet. On the mountain, snow lions are fighting for the triple gem engulfed in a halo of flames. Below that is the round gem of prosperity.**

Opposite: **The statue of the golden yak was erected by the Chinese in Lhasa to mark the anniversary of the "Peaceful Liberation" of Tibet.**

Although likely rebuilt, the Ramoche Temple is said to have been commissioned by Songsten Gampo.

so the Tibetan king was wed to a Nepalese princess, Tritsun, and a Chinese princess, Wencheng. The dowries of both princesses included lavish statues of the Buddha. Songsten Gampo is credited with building the Jokhang and Ramoche temples (which still stand in Lhasa) for the statues, giving his official support to the growing religion, despite opposition from the followers of the Bön religion.

In order for the Buddhist scriptures to be read by the people, Songsten Gampo's minister, Thönmi Sambhota, was sent to India to develop a written script for the language of Tibet. The script they adopted was a form of the writing popularly used in Kashmir in northern India, which they adapted to suit their own needs.

In popular tradition, Songsten Gampo is held as a devout Buddhist who built temples and brought the scriptures to the Tibetan people. He was also a wise ruler who knew that it was in the country's best interests to learn from its powerful neighbors. Songsten Gampo is said to have borrowed techniques from each one of them. From the Hor and Yugur of the north, he copied the books of law; from China he took books of technology and divinatory calculation; India provided the means to translate the holy religion, and in the ancient lands of Sok and Nepal he opened the treasuries of foodstuffs, wealth, and goods for the people.

TRISONG DETSEN (755–797)

In the hundred years following the death of Songsten Gampo, the Buddhist temples fell into disrepair. The animistic religion practiced by the earlier kings was still a strong force in Tibet and its priests were jealous of any support the king might give to Buddhism.

Expansion of the empire resumed under the rule of Trisong Detsen. In 763, Tibetan armies captured the capital of China, which was then at modern Xi'an, and installed their own emperor. But Trisong Detsen is remembered more in Tibetan history for his contributions to Buddhism

The Samye monastery, built under the rule of Trisong Detsen.

than for his military exploits. Trisong Detsen, a Buddhist himself, restored Songsten Gampo's temples, invited Buddhist masters into Tibet, and had new translations of the scriptures made. One of the famous monks he brought to Tibet was a man called Shantarakshita, who is revered by modern Tibetans as the Great Abbot Bodhisattva. A bhodhisattva is someone who has achieved a state of enlightenment but chooses to return to an earthly life to help other people achieve the same state. With Shantarakshita's help, Trisong Detsen gathered enough support to declare Buddhism the state religion.

During this king's reign, the original monastic order was established in Tibet, and the monastery of Samye was built. This angered Bön supporters, who plotted their revenge in an effort to oust the king from the throne.

THE END OF THE EMPIRE

In 815, Trhitsuk Detsen (Relpachen), the last of the great Buddhist kings of the dynasty of Nyatri Tsenpo, came to power. In 821 a peace treaty was signed with China and inscribed on a pillar outside the Jokhang Temple in Lhasa. Prior to this Buddhist scriptures had been written in various languages, but under Relpachen's rule, Sanskrit was chosen as the official religious language, and translation rules were laid down by royal decree.

Pilgrims hope to reach the holiest temple in Tibet, the Jokhang, at least once in their lifetime.

In this way, a new language was created that was more suited to translation and closer to Tibetan, in contrast to earlier translations that were often so literal they were incomprehensible. The progress of Buddhism did not eliminate earlier beliefs, however, and in 836 Relpachen was assassinated by men acting on the orders of his elder brother, Langdarma, a Bön supporter.

Destruction of Buddhist temples and the persecution of Buddhists began immediately following his death. Buddhist scriptures were burned, and monks were forced to leave their calling or flee the country. Buddhism was wiped out almost completely during Langdarma's rule.

After six years of persecution, a Buddhist monk in hiding traveled to Lhasa in disguise and shot Langdarma in the heart with an arrow. The monk escaped, but his action brought about the eventual collapse of the Tibetan empire. Fighting between the potential heirs to the throne split the kingdom into small warring kingdoms. One branch settled in western Tibet and ruled the state of Guge where Buddhism flourished; in the rest of Tibet, Buddhism declined.

Relpachen carried his devotion so far that he became a monk. The gifts and privileges he bestowed on the clergy probably aroused suspicion and led to his assassination.

THE REVIVAL OF BUDDHISM

The rise and fall of small kingdoms and border disputes with the Chinese continued for 300 years. In the 11th century, a group of fugitive monks who had settled in eastern Tibet began secretly restoring the temples and monasteries. Politically, Tibet still consisted of a series of small, peaceful, feudal kingdoms, but religion and learning flourished. Daily life among the various peoples of Tibet became closely involved with their religious observances. Leading priests, called lamas, ruled equally with the princes and kings. This peaceful period of Tibet's history ended in the 13th century with the arrival of Genghis Khan.

Genghis Khan is considered the most powerful leader in Mongol history.

THE MONGOLS

In the 13th century, the Mongol kingdom began to dominate China and Central Asia. Tibet delayed being attacked early in the century by submitting to the Mongol envoys who were sent to Tibet. Unconditional surrender meant sending an annual tribute to the Mongol emperor. But in 1240, no tribute was sent and this was the signal for the Mongol Empire to take an interest in its southern neighbor.

Under Godan Khan, Genghis' nephew, raiding armies were sent into Central Tibet. These attacks were halted when the head of the Sakya order, a Buddhist monastic order established during the revival, was invited to the court of Godan Khan. Legend has it that Sakya Pandita cured Godan's illness, initiated him into Tibetan Buddhism, and helped create a Mongolian alphabet. In return, Godan Khan granted the Sakya movement the regency of Tibet.

This pact with the Mongols gave the Sakya sect power over the other Buddhist orders. The agreement lasted through the reign of Kubla Khan and continued over the next 100 years until the decline of the Mongol Empire.

In 1354, the Sakya movement was displaced by Jangchub Gyeltsin, a secular leader aligned with the Kagyu order. In the absence of any real threat from the Mongol empire, this pattern of secular alignment with the Kagyu order continued for the next 300 years, until the Yellow Hats, a new order of Buddhist monks who were backed by the Mongols, took control.

THE RISE OF THE YELLOW HATS

While all the political wrangling was going on between the various Buddhist sects during the 14th and 15th centuries, a new religious order was emerging. This was the Gelukpa, meaning virtuous, or Yellow Hats. Their philosophy demanded that members take 253 vows of renunciation, including celibacy.

The leader of this sect, Gendun Drub, testified that when he died, his soul would rise in reincarnation to lead the Yellow Hats. In 1578, the third incarnation, Sonam Gyatso, was invited to visit the Mongol ruler who gave him the title Dalai Lama, which means ocean of wisdom. The Mongol Empire had declined to some extent, but Mongolia still existed as a potential threat to rival groups in Tibet. With the backing of neighboring Mongolia, the Yellow Hats entered the political arena, and in 1642 the fifth Dalai Lama, Lobsang Gyatso (1617–1682), became the political and spiritual leader of Tibet.

THE REIGN OF THE DALAI LAMAS

With the support of the Mongol Empire, Lobsang Gyatso, the fifth Dalai Lama, became the first political and spiritual leader of Tibet. He traveled widely, reforming local government and encouraging the development of monasteries. Long term peace led to the development of a sense of national identity, while culture and the economy flourished.

Political wrangling began again on the death of the sixth Dalai Lama. In 1717, a group of Mongols attacked Tibet and war broke out. Tibet was looted until the Manchu Emperor K'ang Hsi intervened and reinstalled the seventh Dalai Lama, making Tibet a protectorate of China.

For the next 200 years, Tibet was ruled by a series of regents and councils under the direction of Chinese governors; the Dalai Lamas took little part in politics. The ninth to the 12th Dalai Lamas died before reaching 18, possibly assassinated. As Tibet entered the 19th century it became xenophobic and closed all its borders to the outside world.

Parading past the Potala Palace, Chinese soldiers celebrate the anniversary of the "liberation" of Tibet.

Before he died, the 13th Dalai Lama issued a warning that Tibet was in danger "from without and within."

CHINESE "LIBERATION"

Tibet spent most of the 19th century closed to outsiders until a short-lived British invasion in 1904. In 1910, the Manchus invaded to reassert Chinese dominance in Tibet. Under the 13th Dalai Lama (1876–1933), Tibet drove the Chinese out of the country in 1911, and Tibet declared its independence.

However, in neighboring China the nationalist and communist parties were vying for power in a struggle that eventually led to civil war. The nationalist government fell in 1949, withdrawing to Taiwan, while the communists took power on the mainland, creating a People's Government Council headed by Mao Zedong.

One of communist China's first foreign policy objectives was to "peacefully liberate Tibet." The Chinese People's Liberation Army entered eastern Tibet in 1950, taking control of two provinces. Tibetan appeals to the United Nations were ignored. Left with no other alternative, the Tibetan government negotiated an agreement with the Chinese under which Tibet was to remain regionally autonomous and the Tibetan people

THE CULTURAL REVOLUTION

In the 1950s, a division began to develop between China's communist leader Mao Zedong and China's intellectuals. Under Mao's dictatorship, the Cultural Revolution was inaugurated as a means to root out the intellectuals who disagreed with the government and its policies. Groups of young Chinese, known as Red Guards, were recruited by the government to roam over China and its satellite states attacking teachers, doctors, and all signs of culture that did not conform with communist ideals. Chinese and Tibetan cultural relics were destroyed and hundreds of thousands of people were killed. The Cultural Revolution did not come to an end until the death of Mao Zedong in 1979. In recognition of the excesses of this period, since 1980 the Chinese have restored many of the old monasteries and trained Tibetan artists to create new religious images. They have also given Tibetans a greater say in their lives.

free to practice their religion under the leadership of the Dalai Lama.

Not long after the agreement was signed, the Chinese government declared that religion was hampering Tibet's progress. The monasteries were closed and monks executed or sent out into the fields to till the soil. The centuries-old Tibetan agricultural system was scrapped in favor of a series of collective farms. Chinese citizens were relocated to Tibet in an effort to populate the area and make it into a prosperous state. The sudden surge in population combined with the inefficient farm system led to famine, while the economy, burdened with unrealistic reorganization and the demands of the occupying forces, collapsed.

Fearing for his life, the Dalai Lama fled to India. Rebellion began when the communists tried to disarm the Khampas, a nomadic warrior tribe. The people of Tibet rose up in protest and thousands were killed.

After Mao's death, China's regime became slightly more liberal. A Chinese delegation sent to Tibet ordered all taxation and religious persecution halted. In 1985 Tibet was opened to foreign tour groups. Exposure to the outside world led to a serious rebellion in 1987. The foreign press were thrown out and sporadic fighting has continued until the present.

GOVERNMENT

POLITICALLY, TIBET IS an autonomous region of China. Therefore, in order to understand exactly how Tibet's government came about, it is necessary to see it as part of the larger government of China.

THE PEOPLE'S REPUBLIC OF CHINA

The People's Republic of China has a written constitution that has been altered several times since the communist party took power in 1949. Under the most recent constitution of 1982, a president is elected for a five-year term by the National People's Congress, the highest organization of state power in the country. The president's role, however, is largely that of a figurehead.

Executive power lies with the State Council, while the military, a powerful political force, is governed by the Central Military Commission.

Opposite: **A Chinese policeman poses with a Tibetan in front of a painted backdrop of modern conveniences.**

Below: **Modern housing built in the traditional style in central Lhasa.**

The two most powerful positions within the executive are held by the premier and by the general secretary of the Communist Party. Decisions affecting the Tibet autonomous area are made in the State Council where there is no representation by delegates from Tibet.

The legislature, or law-passing body of the Chinese government, is the National People's Congress (NPC), which can also amend the constitution and appoint members of the State Council. The NPC consists of deputies elected for a five-year term from the provinces, autonomous regions, and municipalities of China. In effect, the National People's Congress does little more than ratify the decisions of the State Council. Most of the time the Congress is not convened and is represented by a standing committee. Tibetan delegates to the People's National Congress have little or no power to change policy.

LOCAL GOVERNMENT

Tibet is administered as an autonomous region divided into five prefectures, 71 counties, and one municipality—Lhasa. Local governing bodies are the Tibet Communist Party Committee and the People's Government. The party secretary, a post currently held by Mr. Hu Jintao, a Chinese, is commonly regarded as the most powerful local position.

Below this umbrella structure, Tibet is organized into smaller village units where party discussion groups can put forward ideas and suggestions

The exiled Dalai Lama giving a speech to increase international awareness of the situation in Tibet. In 1989 the Dalai Lama was awarded the Nobel Peace Prize.

GOVERNMENT IN EXILE

When the Dalai Lama fled Tibet for India, nearly 100,000 Tibetans joined him in the months that followed. The community of refugees was granted political asylum by the Indian government but was refused international aid for fear of escalating the Cold War, already at its height. The Dalai Lama appealed for international aid on several occasions. Eventually, in 1959, the United Nations demanded "respect for human rights of the Tibetan people." Turning to the Buddhist precepts of patience and endurance, the Dalai Lama established a community of learning in Dharmsala, to wait until the day he can return to his people in Tibet. Monasteries and Tibetan Buddhist schools are currently fully active, allowing people from Tibet and outside to visit and learn. More recently, the Dalai Lama has traveled to various Western countries to urge their governments to bring to a halt what he calls a "cultural genocide."

to improve village life. According to critics, however, village units have little or no power, and effectively Tibet is governed by a massive Chinese bureaucracy whose policies are supported by an enormous military presence.

THE PEOPLE'S JUDICIARY

The highest body in the judicial system is the People's Supreme Court, responsible for upholding the constitution and regulations of the State Council. The 1982 constitution of China guarantees the right of legal defense to those brought to the official law courts. However, the law practiced under the Chinese legal system pertaining to Tibet is very different from the law practiced in other countries. Much that would be handled in the courts is negotiated by the Communist Party at its local meetings. Issues such as minor theft and divorce are dealt with in this way. Trials are held, but in many cases they are for the purpose of setting an example. Often those found guilty are summarily dealt with, leaving no right of appeal.

THE DALAI LAMAS

Before the Chinese invasion in 1951, the Dalai Lama was the supreme religious and political leader of Tibet. He was supported by two prime ministers, one of them a monk and the other a lay person, and a council consisting of four ministers. One of the ministerial posts was invariably reserved for a monk. The Department of Religious Affairs, an ecclesiastical group represented entirely by monks, acted on the same authority as the council of ministers. In the interim periods before the young Dalai Lama took on the leadership of the country, a regent was appointed by the National Assembly in his stead.

The Tibetan National Assembly consisted of 350 members and worked closely with the 60-member Working Committee. These two bodies were responsible for determining national policy. Their conclusions were subject to consideration by the Dalai Lama and his council of religious and political advisors.

CHINESE VS TIBETAN RULE

For many years Tibet existed as an independent state with its own national language, religion, and culture. But in many ways the country was run as a feudal state with little recognition or representation of the people. There was no constitutional guarantee of human rights, and sentences were often harsh and arbitrary.

The Chinese administration of Tibet has built roads, industries, and power stations and encouraged tourism. Tibetans now have a better standard of living than they did under the rule of the Dalai Lama. They have access to consumer goods, television and radio, and limited freedom of worship. Many monasteries have been restored and declared national monuments, and modern homes and offices have been built.

But the same administration encouraged thousands of Chinese settlers to migrate to the region with offers of guaranteed jobs with higher pay, preferential education for their children, and newly-built homes. They have sent thousands of Tibetan children out of the region to schools in Chinese provinces where they have learned to speak Chinese more fluently than Tibetan. Still in exile, the Dalai Lama has made overtures to the Chinese government hoping for some improvement for his people, but most have been rejected.

Loyalty to the Dalai Lama continues despite Chinese discouragement.

ECONOMY

PRIOR TO 1951, Tibet was a self-sufficient, agricultural economy that relied on trading with neighboring tribes for goods such as wool, salt, and barley. There were no roads and the only form of transportation was horse or ass. Wheeled vehicles did not exist in the country until the 20th century and then there were only two cars reserved for the use of the Dalai Lama, which had been dismantled and brought into Tibet on horseback through the Himalayan mountain passes. There was no electricity, no telephone service, no television, no radio, and little contact with the outside world. Modern Tibet is a very different place.

PRE-1959 ECONOMY

When the Chinese assumed authority in Tibet, they discovered an agricultural economy based on small, mobile family units raising cattle and sheep and growing crops. As the seasons changed, families moved with their animals to find more suitable grazing land. A delicate balance existed between this vast inhospitable land and the people who made a living from it.

Opposite: **This factory produces Tibetan medicine to be exported to China.**

Above: **Greenhouses are a relatively new addition to the Tibetan landscape.**

In a country where firewood was not plentiful, animal dung was dried and used as fuel, leaving little or none as crop fertilizer. Population was controlled by the number of people the land could support. The importance of religion in Tibet meant that large numbers of men and women devoted their lives to service in nunneries and monasteries. This traditional economy is still the norm for a large percentage of the Tibetan rural population.

THE ARRIVAL OF THE CHINESE

When the Chinese arrived they banned the barter system, which was the method most Tibetans used to obtain necessary goods, replacing it with Chinese currency. Winter wheat was introduced as the major crop in a land where the economy depended on barley, and small farms were transformed into communes. This created large herds of animals grazing the same small area. As a result of these changes, the soil quickly became exhausted, which led to serious crop failures and periods of starvation.

In 1980, Hu Yaobang, a high-ranking official in the Chinese Communist Party, visited Tibet and was shocked at conditions there. As a result, the communes were disassembled, herds were broken up and redistributed, and the winter wheat policy was abandoned. Cross border trade with Nepal was allowed again, and tourists were granted visas to enter Tibet, bringing valuable foreign currency.

In more recent years, China has begun investing heavily in Tibet and Western China, and policy changes have restored a free market economy.

INVESTMENT IN TIBET'S ECONOMY

China is beginning to undergo the transition from state-run economy to partially free economy. By removing state subsidies, the government hopes to force industries formerly run by the state to become profitable. In addition to this, many of the rural communes have been disbanded in favor of family-run units. Despite attempts at reform through investment programs in the west of China and Tibet, there has been little industrial development. According to recent investment plans, by the year 2000, 10 billion yuan will have been invested in energy, education, transportation, and health care. The Chinese provinces have been instructed to devote funds to industrial projects in Tibet.

The solar radiation observatory at the east Rongbuk glacial basin has recorded a generation rate of 1.8 calories of energy per square centimeter per minute. This is the highest level of solar energy generation in the world.

One of the major areas of investment in the last 10 years has been power plants. Geothermal and hydroelectric plants are running and there are plans to build the world's largest hydroelectric plant at the turning point of the Yarlung Zangbo in the southeast. There is also enormous potential for solar energy and wind energy power. Portable solar energy panels are already widely used for domestic heating and lighting.

Boiling water from primitive solar panels. The strength of the sun in the winter makes solar energy the most logical choice for Tibetans.

YANBAJING

Yanbajing is a hot spring covering an area of six square miles (16 square kilometers). The spring water becomes hot by the process of decay of radioactive elements in the earth's crust. The energy is transferred upwards through the crust through natural faults and eventually finds its way to the earth's surface. In 1976, a geothermal energy power station was built that now supplies the capital city of Lhasa with 8,000 kilowatt hours of energy. In a country that has not exploited any fossil fuels and has little else to power generating stations, this is a very important development.

AGRICULTURE

Tibet is still largely an agricultural economy. Principal crops are grown in the fertile south of the country and include barley, oats, rapeseed, corn, and buckwheat. Legumes such as broad beans and peas, which are useful in refertilizing the soil, are grown in the south. Mustard and many green vegetables are also cultivated. Small amounts of cotton, soybeans, and hemp are grown commercially.

The high altitude and intense sunshine allow for two harvests a year, each giving enormously high yields. As much as 5,350 pounds of barley per acre (6,000 kilograms/hectare) can be harvested as opposed to a normal yield of 1,780 pounds (2,000 kilograms).

Traditional farming methods are common in Tibet, where few farms are fully, or even partially, mechanized.

The introduction of technology has also contributed substantially to the high crop yield. Land once farmed entirely by yak-drawn wooden ploughs is now tilled by tractor and other modern machinery. Irrigation systems and reservoirs have been built as a substitute for the lack of adequate rainfall.

In the past farmers were given quotas and the produce was collected by the regional government for redistribution. Now they are free to make their own contracts and sell to the highest bidder.

Animal husbandry is also practiced widely in Tibet. In the north of the country herders are largely nomadic, moving with their animals in search of fresh grazing land. The yak is the most common animal in these parts, but

YAKS

Yaks are native to the Central Asian plateau. The vast majority of yaks are found in China, Tibet, and the Qinghai Plateau. Wild male yaks are about 6.5 feet (2 meters) high at the shoulder and weigh up to about 2,200 pounds (1,000 kilograms). They are covered with long black or brown hair, and have long horns and a hump at the shoulder.

Domesticated yaks are smaller and their color ranges from black to red or white. They are enormously useful producing rich milk that can be made into cheese and butter; the butter can also be used as fuel. The meat is eaten raw, dried, or roasted. The bones are made into jewelry or utensils and the hide and fur serve as clothes, rope, boats, or tents. A dzo, a cross between a yak and a cow, is a smaller, more docile animal often used to pull ploughs.

goats, sheep, horses, donkeys, and a yak-cow cross called a *dzo* ("ZO") are also kept. Wool from sheep is the most important article of trade for the pastoral nomads.

MINERALS

Recently, a survey was conducted to measure the potential for developing Tibet's mining industry. According to the survey, there are large deposits of minerals in Tibet, including iron ore, coal, oil, shale, manganese, lead, zinc, and graphite. Gold, jade, and other precious and semiprecious stones have also been found. The resources are available for exploitation; it is now a matter of developing Tibet's immature mining industry.

Salt and borax have been collected in small amounts for years, but there is the potential to develop these small-scale industries. The world's largest lithium deposit is in Tibet and uranium deposits have also been found.

Because of the sun's intensity and the long periods of bright sunshine year round, vegetable crops grow to enormous sizes. Potatoes weighing 4.5 pounds (2 kilograms) and cabbages weighing 62 pounds (28 kilograms) have been recorded.

Carpet weaving is an ancient Tibetan craft.

MANUFACTURING

Manufacturing in Tibet is still very much in its infancy. Textiles, especially wool, are the principal items manufactured. A large woollen products factory east of Lhasa supports nearly 1,300 workers, 50% of whom are Tibetan. The factory makes rugs, blankets, and knitwear.

Other manufactured goods include processed leather, chemicals, print works, and electrical equipment, mostly for home consumption. Handicrafts such as appliquéd tents, butter churns, and religious artifacts are sold largely to tourists. Workers engaged in handicraft work receive state subsidies.

THE MILITARY

Viewed as an industry, the military is probably the largest single employer in Tibet. There are approximately 150,000 People's Liberation Army troops in Tibet, with four military camps surrounding Lhasa alone. For the one public airfield there are nine military ones. Intercontinental ballistic missiles are kept at three nuclear bases. Tibet is strategically important for China, giving it a forward base for any potential attack on its neighbors and forming a natural barrier to any invasion or missile attack from that area. Tibet is also used as a nuclear testing site.

FORESTRY

Timber is the largest export from Tibet into China. Although most of Tibet is covered with grasslands, in the valleys to the southeast several species of evergreen and deciduous trees can be found. In fact, there are about 15,616,720 acres (6.32 million hectares) of forest in Tibet. In the tropical zones, camphor and tropical oaks produce valuable hardwoods. The tung tree, which supplies industrial oil, and a lacquer tree that produces varnish are also harvested.

TOURISM

Tibet has been reopened for tourism since 1985. Coinciding with this, the government has allowed the restoration of some monasteries and holy places, generally undertaken by returning monks and their supporters. Still, a largely undeveloped infrastructure cannot support the large numbers of tourists necessary to make tourism a viable industry. It has only been recently that Tibetan cities have been equipped with luxury hotels, bus services, and restaurants. A small craft industry has also been established to cater exclusively to tourists. Cultural and religious items such as prayer wheels and ethnic jewelry are produced.

Tourist and trader bargain over a souvenir. Some Tibetans have begun to make a living selling handicrafts to tourists.

Although tourism will continue to bring in valuable foreign currency, facilitate cultural exchange, and create an infrastructure that is helpful to Tibetans, there is a danger that it will be at the cost of that which Tibetans have been fighting to protect—their ancient culture and religious beliefs.

TIBETANS

ACCORDING TO THE DALAI LAMA, four million of the total Tibetan ethnic group of six million live outside the autonomous region, either in exile or in Chinese provinces. Of the two million people remaining in Tibet, there are several different peoples.

The people who have traditionally inhabited Tibet are thought to be the descendants of a non-Chinese race who came to Tibet from the northeast and intermarried with the Chinese. In addition to these, there are smaller groups of varying ethnic origin, such as the Moinba, who look different and speak different dialects, the Bhotia, who generally live outside Tibet around the Tibet-Nepal border, and the Ladakhi, who now also largely live in eastern Kashmir but who consider themselves Tibetan. Since 1951, there has also been a large influx of Han Chinese who have migrated from the south.

The people of the various geographical areas of Tibet have different legends surrounding their origins: the people of the central valleys claim the southeast as the birthplace of the Tibetans, while aristocratic families believe they originated in the north and northeast of the country, closer to the borders with China. Whatever their origins, Tibetans are generally distinguished by their lifestyle—the Bopa, or settled people of the south and east, and the Drokpa, nomadic people of the Northern Plateau.

Opposite: **Two young Tibetan boys at the Drepung monastery in Lhasa.**

THE BOPA

The Bopa are the farmers and herders who live in the lush valleys of southern and eastern Tibet. Their herds are kept in one place and the mainstay of their livelihood is growing crops. They have been more influenced by the arrival of the Chinese than the Drokpa and are more likely to have elements of Chinese in their language and lifestyle than the nomads.

A Khampa woman. The Khampa, a warrior tribe of the Northern Plateau credited with driving out the Chinese in 1911, are considered Drokpa.

THE DROKPA

While not physically different from their southern compatriots, the Drokpa live a very different kind of life. They live for the most part in tents in the high regions of the Northern Plateau, but they are constantly on the move. They are a dynamic and lively people who still wear traditional Tibetan dress. It is said that they are friendly and hospitable. They are often devout worshippers and are the first to be found at religious occasions, often traveling great distances to the nearest temple or monastery to attend services. With little or no regard for the established legal system, the Drokpa are said to deal out their own justice, which is often harsh.

THE HAN CHINESE

Figures for the total number of Chinese living in Tibet vary enormously from seven million downwards. Whatever the figure, it is high in comparison to the Tibetan population. In fact, in the cities and larger towns the Chinese population exceeds the Tibetan.

Chinese people have many reasons for choosing to live in Tibet. They are guaranteed good jobs with higher pay than they would get elsewhere in China, their children are given priority in education, and they live in modern Chinese-built houses. If they choose to go into business for themselves, they receive state subsidies and tax breaks. The greatest incentive may be that the one-child restriction that applies to Chinese living in other parts of China is lifted in the case of Tibetan Chinese.

THE BHOTIA

Bhot is the name by which Tibet is known to the Nepalese and the Indians. The Bhotia are seasonal nomads who speak Tibeto-Burman dialects and practice Tibetan Buddhism (Lamaism) as their religion. Physically, they resemble Tibetans, and for the most part they consider themselves to be Tibetan even though the large majority of them actually live in the border areas between India and Tibet and Nepal and Tibet. Their houses are built of stone and timber and are often furnished.

Like the Tibetans, the Bhotia depend heavily on the yak for food, clothes, fuel, and tents, as well as implements made from the bones and hoofs. They also raise sheep and goats. Their characteristic dress is similar to the traditional Tibetan style—long woolen clothes with lots of jewelry. The old Tibetan tradition of polyandry (one woman taking more than one husband, usually brothers) is still common, and there is considerable sexual equality between Bhotia men and women.

For many years, until the Chinese relaxed the restrictions on the Tibetan practice of religion, the Bhotia were one of the few peoples who were able to keep the traditions of Tibetan Buddhism alive.

Collecting flowers in the Zanskar Valley, on the border between Tibet and India.

THE LADAKHI

The elaborate headdress of the Ladakhi, inlaid with stones and jewels.

The Ladakhi are another Tibetan group who live outside the borders of Tibet, this time in Kashmir on Tibet's eastern border. There are about 50,000 Ladakhi living on the Ladakh Plateau. The Ladakhi speak a Tibetan dialect and practice Tibetan Buddhism. They are the descendants of Tibetans who moved east out of Tibet and mixed with other ethnic groups, such as the Dards and the Mons of ancient Kashmir. In dress, they are similar to the nomads of northern Tibet with felt boots, leggings, and a woolen or sheepskin greatcoat.

Like the Bhotia, the Ladhaki women often marry all the brothers of one family. Many of the men enter monasteries, joining the sect popularly known in Tibet as the red hats, the rivals of the Lamaists.

The Ladakhi suffered a great deal when the borders of Tibet were closed because they are pastoralists and traders who often crossed the border to trade with Tibet. They continue to suffer as the roads open to modern transportation, which is far more efficient than their yaks. The Ladhaki live very much as the pastoral Tibetans do, farming crops such as cereals that they irrigate by means of terracing and trapping water from mountain streams. The men do most of the ploughing, while the women look after the crops once they have been planted. During the summer most of the men travel with the animals to better grazing lands, just as the pastoral Tibetans do.

Ladhaki homes are built into the sides of mountains in split levels. Houses have flat roofs and are nearly windowless. The family sleep all together on a raised platform at the back. The chuba is the main garment for men, while the women wear a striped skirt and striped apron, woolen leggings, and felt boots. Like Tibetans, Ladhaki women braid their hair to indicate their marital status.

THE LHONBA

Although the Lhonba live in southeastern Tibet, few of them speak Tibetan, preferring their own ancient language, which has no written form. They rely primarily on agriculture for their livelihood, but they also keep animals, produce textiles, and hunt. The Lhonba are particularly fond of smoking and drinking, and like Tibetans they adorn themselves with plenty of jewelry.

Aside from jewelry, the men wear sleeveless jackets made of wool and hats made of bearskin or bamboo. The women wear short blouses with a round neckline and narrow sleeves, and a close-fitting skirt. Unlike most other Tibetan Buddhists, the Lhonba always bury their dead in the ground.

A young Ladakhi woman in Kashmir no longer conforms to Ladakhi modes of dress, preferring to adopt the Kashmir fashion.

THE MOINBA

The Moinba represent a population of about 40,000 distributed primarily in the forested areas around the Moinyu area in southern Tibet. Though they depend on agriculture, they are also engaged in forestry, animal husbandry, and hunting. Their diet consists mainly of the grains they grow: rice, chicken-claw millet, corn, and buckwheat. Moinba houses are built of stones or rocks with a pointed roof that looks like an inverted *V*. They are two to three stories high; the people live upstairs, while the animals are kept downstairs. The Moinba are easily distinguished by their red pulu robe and black felt hat with a brown top, an orange fringe, and a gap at its peak. The women generally wear white aprons at their waist and carry a yak hide on their back to keep out the cold.

A Moinba community on the border between Sichuan province and Tibet.

SOCIAL HIERARCHIES

Tibetan social hierarchies are very complicated and made even more so by the overlay of Chinese values that has permeated society since the 1950s. When the Chinese arrived in Tibet they expected to find a feudal society where an aristocratic class ruled over peasants and artisans. This was largely true but too simple a picture.

Aristocratic Tibetan families traced their descent from the early kings of Tibet originating in the east of the country. Peasants and nomads lived a hard life working for the nobles or tending their own small farms. But mingled with this feudal society, there was a powerful religious order that formed a microcosm of greater Tibetan society.

Estimates put the number of monks and nuns at 20% of the total population before 1950. Within the monasteries, monks were divided by rank and function. Within each sect, monks took on different roles, many of them being more involved with the everyday running of the monastery than religious devotion. In the past, the country was run jointly by the monks and the nobility.

Under the communist regime, monks are no longer subject to the social hierarchies they once were.

49

Today, the number of children allowed to enter nunneries and monasteries is restricted by the government.

But unlike other feudal societies where one's rank at birth remained unchanged throughout one's lifetime, the monastic system allowed for a degree of social mobility. Most families, if they could afford it, dedicated one of their children to the monasteries, where they were fed, clothed, educated, and employed. The priesthood offered the children of the poor the opportunity to rise in society to become revered and learned scholars or community leaders.

In modern times a new social hierarchy exists. The nobility are still present and for the most part are the wealthier families, but the real elite in society now are the Chinese, who hold most of the good jobs in the administration.

THE ABOMINABLE SNOWMAN

Sightings of the yeti, as the abominable snowman is also known, are rare, but myths, legends, and stories of its existence abound throughout the world. The yeti is supposed to live in caves in the high reaches of the Himalaya. A research society in China has recently published a report on the creature. According to the report, the yeti is approximately 6.25 feet (1.9 meters) in height and covered with thick, long, smooth fur that ranges in color from white to dark brown. Yeti forage among the trees and roots for food, and catch and eat small mammals. Although they walk upright, they are said to be very agile in trees. The footprints that have been discovered indicate that they have very large feet and go barefoot.

Stories of contact and capture have been told but each time the yeti have managed to escape before they could be brought before witnesses. In 1985, the Chinese research society thought they had caught a yeti, but it turned out to be a rare macaque, 3.5 feet (1.06 meters) tall, weighing 203 pounds (92.5 kilograms). The yeti may well be related to the mythic American creature known as Big Foot.

REFUGEES

When the Dalai Lama fled Tibet in 1959, thousands of people followed and settled with him in India or moved to other countries such as Nepal and Switzerland, as part of refugee settlement programs. Over the years the Chinese government has agreed to allow several delegations from the Dalai Lama into Tibet to carry out studies of the state of the people, but the Dalai Lama himself has never returned. Tibetans are free to return to Tibet if they have the courage, but on their entry visa they must write that they are Chinese citizens.

For many years the United States refused to accept Tibetans as political refugees, maintaining its agreement of noninterference in China's domestic affairs. But more recently, Tibetans have been granted entrance into the United States. In 1993, 1,000 Tibetans landed on U.S. soil, settling in small groups in cities such as New York and Minneapolis. They are not given refugee status, so they get no federal support, but Americans who sympathize with their plight have helped them to find work.

Despite living outside Tibet for so long, these women still worship in the traditional Tibetan way.

Taking a break from a long day's work over a cup of tea.

TRADITIONAL DRESS

The national dress of Tibet is the *chuba* ("CHOO-pa"), a long-sleeved loose cloak worn by both men and women. The cloak is wrapped around the body and fastened at the waist with a colorful belt. The blousy front of the chuba becomes the repository for everything from groceries to worldly goods. Underneath the chuba, a variety of shirts, vests, and jackets are worn to keep out the cold. Long woolen breeches are tucked into knee-high felt boots. Women wear long, black, sleeveless dresses and blouses, and an apron of brightly colored horizontal stripes.

In the past, one's dress was dictated by one's social standing. Nomadic men wore a shorter version of the chuba made of sheepskin, and women wore a much longer version. Exact details of men's dress were laid down by decree. During the winter, from December to April, all lay and ecclesiastical officials had to wear fur hats and cloaks. After April no one could wear fur even if it was freezing!

The majority of the people in Tibet still wear traditional dress.

Hats were once a very important feature of Tibetan dress. People were generally identified by the kinds of hats they wore, and as hats differed according to geographical region, a person from the south could be easily distinguished from a person from the north.

Women's hats were often made of a wooden frame covered in cloth and ornamented with precious stones. The number and size of the stones indicated her wealth. On some occasions these hats are still worn.

Today, hats are often made of fur and brocade and shaped like a flowerpot with flaps at the ears. More commonly seen in the towns are two types of men's hats: trilbies, a soft felt syle, and homburgs.

Jewelry is an important element in both men's and women's dress in Tibet. Most women carry a prayer wheel, which they rotate as they walk. Over their clothes they wear silver amulets believed to protect them from harm, coral and turquoise beads, a rosary, and silver earrings and bracelets. Ladakhi women wear an elaborate headdress covered in stones and turquoise beads that extends down the length of their backs. Men often carry a tiny statue of a lama, a prayer wheel or a rosary, and wear one earring.

53

LIFESTYLE

THE LIFESTYLE OF THE TIBETAN PEOPLE has undergone many changes over the last 40 years. In the cities and towns, traditional lifestyles based on farming, bartering, and Buddhism have given way to Chinese customs. But as the Chinese administration relaxes its laws regarding worship, the open practice of Buddhism and the restoration of temples and monasteries are increasing. Still, the government hopes that as the standard of living is raised, the Tibetan people will no longer be governed by their religious beliefs.

CITY LIFE

There is really only one settlement in Tibet large enough to be called a city. Lhasa has a population of about 150,000, 70% of whom are Han Chinese. The majority of the Chinese work in the administration of the country or are members of the military force.

Local people are engaged in trade, arts and crafts, and numerous other activities. Many of the ancient religious sites that

were badly damaged during the Cultural Revolution are being restored at government expense; this project employs returned monks and craftsmen. During religious festivals cityfolk and countryfolk meet at the Jokhang Temple, the religious and cultural center of the old city. The temple is surrounded by the market where nomads and foreign and local traders lay out their wares.

In the new part of Lhasa, both Chinese and Tibetans live in work units— blocks of flats in a walled compound with a large gateway. Tibetans in the

Above: **A traditional Tibetan house in the town of Nyalam.**

Opposite: **Religion plays a large role in the everyday lives of Tibetans.**

55

Among the nobility one brother in a family always joined the priest-hood and passed his rank in the government down through his brothers' son. In that way each noble family retained a role both in the secular part of government and in the religious one.

old city live for the most part in whitewashed stone houses of two or three stories with black framed windows that look out on narrow streets and are sheltered by elaborately carved, overhanging eaves. People in both parts of the city now have electricity, primitive plumbing, and refuse facilities. Big, expensive Chinese department stores, where manufactured goods are available, sit alongside traditional small shops selling local produce and handicrafts, giving shoppers a wide choice of goods.

LIFE IN THE COUNTRY

In the valleys of the south and southeast, villages may consist of one or two farmsteads, each supporting one family. The farmhouses are single-story, quadrangular buildings with an open courtyard inside. The entrance leads to the courtyard, which is surrounded by the family's living quarters, storage rooms, barns, and pens for the animals. The flattened roof is used for the storage of fuel (yak dung and brushwood). Streams of flags fly around the house, each one representing a prayer. As the wind blows, the prayer is repeated, bringing good fortune to the family. Farmland often stretches for several acres, depending on the size of the family. The variety of crops planted depends on the climate—barley, oats, apples, and pears in the harsher climates and wheat, apricots, and peaches in the warmer climates. Animals are very important in the village communities; there are few communities where people do not spend part of their time with the herds in search of new pastures.

Traditionally, all the brothers in one family shared one wife and the eldest brother was considered the father of the children. This maintained smallholdings and protected the patrilineal inheritance. In most rural families at least one child left home to join a religious order.

LIFE ON THE NORTHERN PLATEAU

The nomads live in the open plains of the Northern Plateau, moving north in the summer and returning south in the winter. Their tents are made from yak fur that has been transformed into thick waterproof felt by continuous soaking, drying, and beating. The tents are stretched over a wooden frame and held down with ropes. But most of the young people prefer to sleep outside in the open or among the flocks of sheep to keep warm.

Individual nomad communities are large, consisting of several families. They are very self-sufficient, only occasionally coming into settled areas to trade or to attend religious festivals. The nomads provide much of Tibet's meat in the form of mutton, lamb, and yak meat. They exchange the meat for tea, which is mostly imported from China, and *tsampa* ("tsam-PA"), the Tibetan staple food made from roasted barley flour, tea, and butter.

The men spend most of their time away from the camp tending the animals, while the women stay close to the tents.

Nomads often live in communities of three or four families.

57

A tent like this one can take more than a year to complete.

The work of making cloth, curing hides, spinning wool, cooking, and drying the meat for the winter are all carried out by the women. Men and women alike carry a slingshot that they often use to control wandering animals or to fight off wild animals. They rarely hunt or eat wild animals, preferring to eat their domestic animals. Primitive rifles and throwing spears are other nomad weapons. The men all carry a large, elaborate, multipurpose knife.

LIFE IN THE MONASTERIES

In the centuries before the arrival of the Chinese, thousands of boys (approximately one-fifth of the male population) and girls, as young as 5 and 6 years old, were sent to live in the monasteries. The nuns and monks all took a vow of celibacy along with scores of other renunciations, although it was quite customary for men and women to leave and marry, or to join after a period of married life.

Schooling began almost immediately after arrival. Depending on their display of aptitude, monks joined one branch or another of the monastery. Those who showed an intellectual disposition would continue to study, perhaps going on to become a lama, while others might become craftsmen or cooks, gardeners or policemen. The brighter students were educated for 25 years, periodically taking examinations in the form of debates with their teachers. For the nuns there was little chance of intellectual advancement. Their role was usually in the physical administration of the monastery.

Life in the Monasteries

Monasteries became important theological colleges, medical schools, and centers of art and culture. Running businesses or owning land was very profitable as monasteries were free from taxation.

The Tibetan monasteries are currently being renovated, so becoming a monk is still a prospective career. Nevertheless, the numbers of monks and monasteries is strictly limited (1,400 monasteries and 34,000 monks and nuns), and children under the age of 18 are forbidden from entering a religious order.

Since the government has put a cap on the number of monks and nuns, these young monks at Ganden Monastery will have to train especially hard to take on the responsibilities of the decreasing number of lamas.

59

LIFE IN EXILE

Tibetans have been given refuge in many parts of the world, especially in the states bordering Tibet, but the most important Tibetan community is at Dharmsala in India. Several thousand refugees fled to India with the Dalai Lama in 1959 and settled in a former hill station in the mountains. Over the years, temples, monasteries, schools, a medical college, an Institute for the Performing Arts, a library, and a museum dedicated to Tibetan culture have all been built to cater to the needs of the growing population. At the school there are as many as 1,300 pupils of all ages ranging from babies to young adults newly arrived from Tibet.

The refugees are poor by Western standards, often living in one room in a mud house with little or no sanitation. They are employed in craft centers, manufacturing traditional Tibetan carpets and jewelry, as well as T-shirts and bumper stickers with mottoes about Tibetan freedom.

Scattered around other areas of India and Nepal, there are more than 36 Tibetan refugee colonies. Most of these communities rely primarily on agriculture, but many have developed flourishing carpet industries, in some cases running large export businesses. Tibetan refugees are gradually absorbing the culture of their adopted country. Children find it necessary to speak local languages rather than Tibetan in order to pass their exams. There is now a third generation of refugees who have never lived in Tibet, and as time passes there is less likelihood of them ever being able to return.

WOMEN

For centuries Tibetan society was a highly mobile one. As a result, men and women were often separated for months at a time, the men going off with the herds and the women remaining at the camp or village to look after their crops and their families. Consequently, women spent part of the year in charge of the household and became very independent, both economically and socially. Still, positions of power in the community and in business were held by men, and only men could become lamas. The Dalai Lama's government, local administrators, and village chieftains were all men.

A wife was responsible for running the household, negotiating with traders, and handling money. She often owned property that she could count on keeping even in the event of divorce.

Today, young Tibetan women are more likely to resemble their Chinese counterparts than their own mothers, particularly in areas like Lhasa where the Chinese have a strong influence. Schoolchildren are taught to conform to Chinese ideals of sexual behavior, dress, and marriage, which are very different from those of traditional Tibet. For many years, any kind of adornment, including plaits in the hair, was frowned on and in some cases forbidden, despite its social and religious importance to the Tibetans. Marriages are controlled by the work unit, which grants licenses based on Chinese criteria. Tibetan women are limited to two children and one husband only, a policy that deprives them of the status they once held as mothers and wives. Application to the work unit must also be made in order for a woman to travel, to bear a child, or to study. Women now have the right to hold office, but few Tibetans, either women or men, hold any positions in the bureaucracy, which is dominated by the Chinese.

Traditionally, Tibetan women were more independent than their Chinese counterparts.

Snowfall during the time when the bride is on her way to her husband's home is considered very unlucky.

MARRIAGE

The traditional Tibetan wedding begins with the choosing of an auspicious day for the event. When the day finally arrives, the groom's family send for the bride, who must appear unwilling to go with them. She is

accompanied by members of her family, but no one who has been recently bereaved must accompany her. The bride pretends to refuse to go into the house of the groom until she is offered a pail of yak milk by her future mother-in-law. When the ceremony is over, the parents and the bride and groom receive visitors at the groom's house. They wear traditional silk chubas reserved especially for this special day and greet the guests as they file past. Each guest brings six silk scarves, which are presented to each of the parents and the bride and groom. Red paper packets containing money are also common gifts. Yak dung, the main fuel of the Tibetans, and a pail of water decorated with butter are kept outside the door, symbolizing fertility.

Once the formalities are complete, the party, which can last up to six days, begins. Meals are served at regular intervals and Tibetan beer is served.

For the Tibetan Chinese, arranged marriages, subject to parental consent, are very common. Country girls often take older city husbands in order to get a permit to live in the city. Secular monogamy, adopted in the late 1920s, and small families are the Chinese norm, although there was never the one-child policy that existed in the rest of China.

HAVING A FAMILY

The policy limiting children to one per couple is relaxed for the "ethnic minorities," as the Chinese call groups like the Tibetans, and for Chinese people settling in Tibet. However, having any more than two children is penalized: the third and consecutive children get no food ration until they are 18 and no free medical care or education. Since Tibetans are mostly poor, this is a serious liability.

Since the Chinese lifted the ban on religious practice, newborn babies are once again taken to the lama in a traditional name-giving ceremony. During the times when there were no lamas or monks to carry out these duties no one knew how to name their children, and so children acquired some peculiar names. Many were named in the order of their place in the family. Others were named after the day of the week on which they were born. Others were given ugly names in the hope that it would keep any irritated ancestor spirits from claiming the child before its time.

Above: **An extended Tibetan family gathers together for a day in the country.**

Opposite: **Mother and daughters-in-law in their front yard. Their dress indicates that they are Yellow Hat Buddhists.**

63

DEATH RITUALS

Tibetan Buddhists believe that death signifies the departure of the soul from the body, rendering the body a lifeless shell. If the soul has not reached a state of enlightenment, it will be reincarnated in a new body. It is important that Tibetans contribute to the cycle of life and rebirth in order to give back the lives that they have taken—to kill any living thing even for food is a sin. Sky burial is a funeral rite that allows Tibetans to make atonement. In sky burial, the body is carried up to a place high in the mountains where it is cut up into pieces and left for the eagles and vultures. In this way the body provides food for a soul undergoing another incarnation on earth. Skilled men are hired to do this job, as no one wants a relative's body to be left uneaten.

Since the opening of the borders, tourists eager for any new experience go to watch the sky burials, angering many Tibetans for whom this is a sacred ritual and not a photo opportunity. Recently, tourists have been banned from the sites, although some tour operators are planning to set up viewing platforms with telescopes on neighboring peaks.

Another common burial ceremony, reserved primarily for paupers and children, is river burial, where the remains of the body are carried to a river so that they might provide food for fish. Fishing in these sacred rivers, as some Chinese people like to do, is a double insult both to the soul that is incarnated as the fish and to the body of the person it has eaten.

People who are highly honored, such as lamas, are cremated, and in some cases, the cremated remains are divided and sent to various monasteries to be interred in stupas or mausoleums.

Burial in the hard, rocky ground is very rare except for the Lhonba, a group of pastoral Tibetans living in southeast Tibet, who bury their dead in the ground without exception.

EDUCATION

Before the arrival of the Chinese there was no universal education in Tibet. Most formal education took place in the monasteries or by private tutors for the noble families. A basic program of education is now available for all children. In the more heavily populated areas where there are many Chinese settlers, Tibetan and Chinese children attend different primary schools and are taught in their mother tongue with a few hours of instruction in the other language each week.

A public examination for places in middle school is taken at the age of 12. A pass in the Chinese language is essential in order to obtain a place, as Chinese is the medium of instruction, so many Tibetan children are at a disadvantage competing with Chinese children. Nevertheless, the quality of education has improved since the Chinese invasion, and by 1990 there were three new institutes of higher learning, 14 special secondary schools, 64 ordinary secondary schools, and 2,380 elementary schools.

Top: **A Lhasa primary school.**

Bottom: **Students take part in a lesson at a "grass-land school" designed for children who live too far from town to participate in the established educational system.**

Checking the pulse is one of the most effective ways of determining whether or not the life force is in equilibrium.

MEDICINE

As late as the 1950s Tibetan medicine was as much an aspect of religion as it was science. Heinrich Harrer, an Austrian writer who lived in Tibet for seven years, reported that there was no surgery whatsoever in Tibet while he was there. Illnesses were treated as a matter of the spirit rather than of the body. Before the eighth century a form of surgery was practiced in Tibet, but it was banned after the Chinese emperor's mother died during an operation.

Medicine

Traditional Tibetan medicine is based on three humors, wind, bile, and phlegm, rather like the medieval European system. The Tibetan doctor relies heavily on reading the pulse of the patient and analyzing the urine to determine whether there is too much or too little of each one of the humors. Astrology plays a large part in curing the sick as well. The doctor takes careful note of the stars dominating the patient's birth and those dominating at the time of illness before making a diagnosis. Once a diagnosis has been made, the illness is treated with wild herbs that are collected and dried by the monks. Other treatments may include the ingestion of the saliva or urine of holy men, while objects once owned by holy people are often used to prevent illness.

Acupuncture (inserting needles into bodily tissues at particular points) is also used as a cure. Like the Chinese, the Tibetans believe that a life essence flows through the body, keeping the bodily functions in balance. Illness can be brought on if the life essence is prevented from running its course. Acupuncture, acupressure, and moxabustion (burning incense against the skin) are used to restore the healthy flow.

When the Dalai Lama fled in 1959, many skilled Tibetan doctors went with him and a medical school was soon established in Dharmsala. Today Tibetan herbal cures are a main export item in the frail economy of the exiles. The Chinese have recognized the value of Tibetan medicine and have left medical centers in Tibet intact. The medical school in Lhasa has expanded, and the government has sponsored research into the effectiveness of traditional herbal cures.

Rabies is widespread in Tibet, and the Chinese authorities have campaigns to shoot stray dogs. To Tibetans this is the unnecessary killing of a soul—sending it back to be reincarnated before its natural time.

RELIGION

BUDDHISM CAME TO TIBET from India and China in stages, replacing an earlier shamanistic religion called Bön. Buddhism in Tibet is a more integral part of people's lives than what is typical among religious people elsewhere. Although the majority of Tibetans are Buddhist, there is also a small Muslim population who have been settled in Tibet for many years. For many years in China all religion was proscribed, and thus Chinese people were prohibited from practicing any form of religion. But in today's more liberal climate, the Han Chinese in Tibet may be rediscovering their own forms of Buddhism, Taoism, and Christianity.

THE BÖN RELIGION

Bön existed before any form of writing emerged in Tibet, so its earliest origins are unknown. The word *Bön* is the Tibetan name for Tibet, and although the Bön religion still exists in Tibet, it is very different from the early forms. In its earliest stages, the Bön religion was a simple form of animism the main function of which was to protect people from hostile spiritual forces. Ancestral spirits, earth, water, and heavenly spirits had to be appeased with magical rites. Shamans, people with special magical powers, could protect people from these spirits.

As the Buddhist doctrines trickled through the borders, offering competition to the established religion, the Bön religion evolved, taking on new complexities.

Above: **Prayer flags are one of the most common sights in Tibet. Each time the wind blows, stirring the flag, a prayer is released, bringing good fortune.**

Opposite: **The Jokhang Temple is considered the holiest temple in Tibet.**

BUDDHISM

Tibetan Buddhism differs from other forms of Buddhism in that it has retained a large element of the shamanism and magic of Bön. Like all other Buddhist groups, Tibetan Buddhists believe that human existence can be frustrating due to intellectual bewilderment or emotional confusion. In order to escape this kind of suffering, a state of enlightenment is sought where the problems and suffering of the world are no longer harmful. There are three ways to achieve enlightenment: the lesser path, or Hinayana; the greater path, or Mahayana; and the diamond path, or Tantrayana.

HINAYANA This is the way of life adopted by the majority of people in Tibet. The ordinary route to enlightenment is based on the will to achieve nirvana, a state of enlightenment where all desire is transcended, for the individual's own sake. To achieve a state of nirvana, a prescribed school of thought, or path, must be followed: for the Hinayanists it is the "Lesser Way."

To get on this path one must make a commitment to take refuge in the Three Jewels—the Buddha, the Dharma, and the Sangha. This means that a Buddhist's life should be dedicated to enlightenment, symbolized by the Buddha himself, and to adherence to the Dharma, a set of laws established by Buddha. The Sangha is the refuge one takes in the community of people committed to enlightenment, a Buddhist religious community, or monastery.

In childhood, Tibetan Buddhists make a commitment to the Three Jewels in the presence of a lama. They repeat this commitment regularly throughout their lives, rather in the way that some Christian children are brought into the church at the age of 7 and then confirmed in their belief at age 13.

THE MAHAYANA Mahayanists seek to achieve the highest stage of nirvana not only for themselves, but for the sake of all living things. Their goal is to become a bodhisattva. The bodhisattva refrains from entering nirvana in order to guide others on the path to enlightenment. They must show generosity, ethics, tolerance, energy, and wisdom. Enlightened bodhisattvas have cleared their mind of all false ideas and can see the world as it really is. After reaching this state, they help other people achieve the same state.

Compassion for others, demonstrated by the bodhisattva, is central to Tibetan Buddhism. It can be heard in the repeated prayer *om mani padme hum* ("OM-MAN-ee-PAD-may-HUM"). Prior to the Chinese invasion, the walls and hillsides of Tibet were covered with the words of this prayer.

The prayer om mani padme hum *is translated as follows: om (the sound of nature), mani (jewel), padme (lotus), hum (so be it). Jewel in the Lotus is one of the many names for the Buddha.*

Prayers painted on rocks are only one testament to the importance of religion in Tibet.

THE TANTRAYANA Similar to Mahayanists, Tantrayanists seek personal enlightenment to show compassion for others. But this path to enlightenment is more complex. Each stage of enlightenment on this path is represented by a god. As Tantrayanists move to the next stage, they call on the god representing that stage to help them. Using yoga, Tantrayanists channel their energy towards the nature of this god. Tibetan temples were once covered in paintings depicting these deities, some of them calm and benign, others fierce and angry, all of them representing aspects of this path to enlightenment. Through meditation and yoga Tantrayanists eventually see a special clear light that ordinary people can only see in the few hours before death.

BARDO Tibetans believe that after death the spirit passes through the world of bardo. It is here that those who have achieved enlightenment can see the clear light indicating their ascent to nirvana. Nirvana, or liberation, means that the spirit has finally been released from the cycle of death and rebirth.

Bardo consists of seven stages, each subdivided into seven more, so that the soul has 49 days in which to wander in bardo seeking the clear light. At some stage during those 49 days, the unenlightened will be drawn back into the world and born again, or reincarnated as another creature.

DAILY WORSHIP

After 1959, all displays of religious faith were prohibited in Tibet. It was not until the 1980s that religious persecution began to ease. Timidly at first, and then more openly, people returned to their old ways. Every home once had its own shrine, and these began to reappear with photographs of the Dalai Lama as the centerpiece.

A pilgrim making his way through the streets of Lhasa to the Jokhang Temple in a series of prostrations.

Prayer wheels also began to reappear. Once these hand-held wheels would have been carried by everyone. Outside the temples there would once have been rows of huge wheels that people would spin as they passed, reciting the prayer as it emerged from the wheel. These too are being restored.

People are beginning once again to make pilgrimages to holy places. Some people make the entire journey in a series of prostrations, marking the spot where their head lay and standing on that spot before falling again. Some people travel hundreds of miles in this way. Even more devout people make journeys proceeding according to their width, rather than their height.

The pilgrims and worshippers bring gifts of incense and flowers, or butter to fuel the lamps in the temple. Some people bring seven bowls of pure water, which symbolizes their pure self.

Some superstitious practices are returning as well, such as rubbing parts of the body on holy relics to cure an ailment and putting pins in the cloth of a holy statue in the hope that it will sharpen the intelligence.

THE WHEEL OF LIFE

Complex diagrams of the wheel of life are often drawn on the walls of Buddhist temples. The wheel shows the universe without beginning or end and the countless world systems that exist within this universe. Within each world system there are six basic forms of life: human, animal, celestial, titan, ghosts, and denizens of hell.

In the center of the picture are a pig, a snake, and a rooster, which represent ignorance, hatred, and desire. These are the things that keep the spirit entrapped in the wheel of life. The individual spirit has no beginning in the wheel of life, it has always existed and has been reborn many times over. The way in which the spirit has conducted itself in one incarnation determines its reincarnation in the next life. The next circle shows the

One example of the Wheel of Life sits atop the Jokhang Temple.

spirits of those who have almost achieved enlightenment but have been thrown back down into hell because of a failure of the will. The six realms of existence into which the spirit is continually reborn are depicted in the next ring, while the outermost ring shows the 12 stages of life from ignorance in the previous life, to ageing and death in the next.

LAMAS

Lama translated literally means "superior one." A lama, like a bodhisattva, is someone who has achieved a state of enlightenment and becomes a spiritual teacher to help others along the same path. Lamas are important because as the student seeking enlightenment moves on to each higher level, he is assisted by a lama who shows him the nature of the next stage.

Most monasteries have one or two holy men who have chosen not to go to nirvana but to be reincarnated so that they may help more people to a state of enlightenment. The two most important lamas in Tibet are the Dalai Lama and the Panchen Lama.

THE PANCHEN LAMA

The Panchen Lama is second only to the Dalai Lama in religious authority. The first incarnation of the Panchen Lama took place in the 14th century and continued unhindered until the death of the ninth in 1937.

It was not until 1950, 13 years after the death of the ninth Dalai Lama, that two Tibetan candidates were discovered. Relations between the Chinese and the Tibetans had been deteriorating, so when the Chinese put forward a candidate, the Tibetans feared the political situation would worsen if he was turned down. Despite the fact that traditional tests were not administered, the Chinese candidate gradually came to be accepted as the true incarnation. He was taken to Beijing at the age of 14 and his training and education were both subjected to Chinese influence.

After the Dalai Lama fled Tibet in 1959, the Panchen Lama was declared the political and spiritual leader of Tibet. When he was allowed to return to Tibet, he declared his allegiance to the Dalai Lama and was arrested. He spent years in Chinese prisons and was only pardoned in the late 1970s. His death in 1989 incited a search for his reincarnation. In 1995, the Dalai Lama proclaimed the discovery of the 6-year-old Panchen Lama. The Chinese authorities, annoyed by the proclamation, took the boy into their custody, announcing their intention to educate him in their own way.

Opposite: **The incarnation of a Tibetan lama in Darjeeling, India.**

Below: **The present Dalai Lama (left) and the 10th Panchen Lama both about age 24 here.**

THE SEARCH FOR THE TRUE LAMA

Tibetan Buddhism is divided into several sects, distinguished locally by the color of the hats they wear. One sect, the black hats or Kagyupa, is still struggling over the identity of its 17th leader. In 1992, the son of a Tibetan nomad whose birth had been accompanied by wondrous signs, was found. The child, named Ugen Thinley, now age 11, was enthroned at a monastery in Lhasa with the Dalai Lama's approval (he too had seen visions confirming the identity of the child). But in 1994, a second child turned up in the protection of a former regent of the lama. Of Tibetan origin, and two years older than Ugen Thinley, this child is said to have identified himself to his parents when he was 3 years old.

The adherents of the two reincarnations accuse the other of being agents of the Chinese who, they say, seek to get their hands on the extensive wealth of the Kagyupa sect. The Kagyupa's main monastery is now in Rumtek in India. In 1995, the Chinese began a new campaign to try to turn the Tibetan people against the Dalai Lama by claiming that Ugen Thinley is the natural leader of Tibetan Buddhism because the Kagyupa sect was founded before the Gelukpa sect. Tibetans fear that Ugen Thinley will be manipulated the way the Panchen Lama was.

FINDING THE INCARNATIONS

Discovering the rebirth of a lama is not an easy affair. Unusual remarks made prior to a lama's death are duly noted as a possible clue to the location of the rebirth, but it could be days or years before the child is found.

When the 13th Dalai Lama died, no clear indications were left, so the lamas waited for a sign. As the embalmed body of the 13th Dalai Lama lay in state, his head began to turn in one direction. This sent the searchers to a lake where visions are said to appear on the water's surface. After meditating at the lake the lamas saw a vision of a green roofed building near a temple. They found the building in northeast Tibet, where a child recognized one of the Dalai Lama's followers and some of his possessions. The lamas had to ask the Chinese for permission to take the child and were forced to pay a high ransom for him. The child, the present Dalai Lama, immediately moved to the monastery in Lhasa where he lived until his exile in 1959.

Prayer wheels outside the Ganden Monastery. Each time the wheels are spun, the spinner is blessed.

RELIGIOUS SYMBOLS

Hung from roofs of buildings, trees, and poles, prayer flags are the most prevalent religious symbol in Tibet. As the wind blows, the prayer printed on the flag is released, bringing luck and prosperity to the devoted.

Swastikas are common symbols of both Tibetan Buddhism and the Bön religion. Drawn clockwise, the Swastika is the Buddhist symbol of good fortune. Drawn counterclockwise it represents the Bön symbol of good fortune.

The bell and *dorje* ("DOOR-jay"), a stick used to hit the bell, together form another common religious symbol. The dorje represents a thunderbolt and the bell's chime is said to drive away evil.

The lotus flower is a common inclusion in Tibetan Buddhist paintings and murals because it symbolizes nirvana, the state of complete enlightenment. A representation of two fish, often painted on the walls of houses, symbolizes the souls of people liberated by religious faith and able to swim freely.

Pilgrims on long journeys can often be seen carrying mani stones, small stones with the prayer *om mani padme hum* carved or painted on them. When they reach the temple or holy place, they lay the stones in huge piles outside the entrance.

Sculptures of butter and tsampa are considered holy food and are presented to the temples during festivals. The sculptures are cones constructed out of colored food and studded with discs made from butter.

The Buddhist cosmos is often depicted in mandalas, which are complex patterns of squares and circles showing the path to enlightenment. Mandalas are used by monks to guide themselves to the next stage of enlightenment. Monks skilled in making mandalas sometimes spend weeks creating one out of sand on the ground outside the monastery, a fitting demonstration of the impermanence of all things.

Mani stones are piled outside the temple, representing the pilgrims who travel there every year.

LANGUAGE

TIBET REMAINED an isolated country in every sense of the word for centuries. Because of this, Tibetan is unlike many other languages, which have been influenced by foreign films or television. Tibetan is believed to belong to a tiny family of languages known as Tibeto-Burmese spoken in the Tibet Autonomous Region, large areas of Sichuan, Yunnan, Gansu, and Qinghai provinces in China, and parts of Sikkim, Ladakh, and Nepal. Although there are several dialects of Tibetan spoken around Tibet, they are all mutually intelligible. Since the arrival of the Chinese, Tibetan has become a second language for children sent to China for their schooling. English was never widely spoken in Tibet and is unknown outside of the few large towns. As the need for international communication increases, many people begin to see English as a means of bettering their lives, so a few English-language schools are in operation.

Above: **A tale of the Buddha painted on a monastery wall.**

Opposite: **A young pilgrim chants the holy scriptures for money on a street in Lhasa.**

WRITING

There are four different ways of writing the 30 consonants and four vowels of the Tibetan alphabet, depending on the occasion. The most stylized—the equivalent of English capital letters—is called *U-chen* ("you-CHEN") and used in printed text. *U-me* ("you-MAY") is more flowing and ornate and used for inscriptions or formal letters. The two other scripts are simpler and are used in everyday writing. If two words have the same sound but different meanings, which is common, one can be written with an extra consonant to indicate the difference.

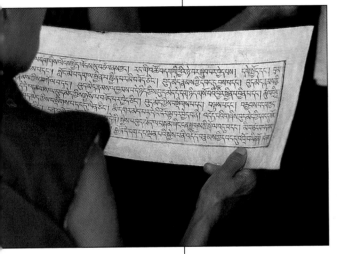

A page of the ancient scriptures being read aloud by a young monk in training.

SPOKEN TIBETAN

Spoken Tibetan is closer to European languages than to Chinese because it is phonetic, meaning that the alphabet represents the sounds of the letters rather than the meaning of the word. Most Tibetan words have only one or two syllables, but prefixes and suffixes can be added to alter pronunciation or meaning. The word order of a Tibetan sentence is always subject - object - verb.

In Tibetan there is no equivalent to yes or no. Instead the final part of the verb is repeated either affirmatively or negatively.

There are three basic tenses in Tibetan that correspond to the English past, present, and future tenses. Each verb consists of two words, the first indicating the meaning and the second showing the tense, so that *nyo ge ray* ("neo-ge-RAY") means buying or going to buy, while *nyo song* ("neo-SONG") means bought.

HONORIFICS

Until the arrival of the Chinese, Tibetan society was highly hierarchical with clearly defined social positions. This feudal nature is reflected in a series of honorifics used to show respect. When addressing a person of a higher rank, the speaker added a single-syllabled prefix to certain words. Often a completely different set of words was used when speaking to, or even referring to, priests or people of very high rank. When the Cultural Revolution began, all signs of feudalism were considered reactionary and banned. Since then the practice of honorifics, especially among younger people and city dwellers, has largely died out.

Tibetan holy books are preserved and stored very carefully. To the Tibetan Buddhist, these books are sacred.

MANTRAS

Mantras are special forms of language that have a ritual or magic quality. Written in Sanskrit, they are ancient prayers thought to precipitate and condense energies. They generally begin and end with two very special sounds: *om,* which is considered the "seed sound," the origin and essence of all life, and *hum,* which directs the energies of the person praying. Uttered correctly, the sound *om* can put the individual in tune with all the voices of the world, all the sounds of nature, and the structure of the cosmos. People spend a lifetime learning to iterate the sound correctly.

The most common Tibetan mantra is *Om mane padme hum.* It is the name of one of the states of the Buddha and translates as "Jewel in the lotus." This mantra is often written on stones outside the monasteries, printed on prayer flags and prayer wheels, or written on tiny pieces of paper and worn in lockets to protect the wearer.

Another of the oldest Buddhist mantras is *Om gate gate paragate parasamgate bodhih svaha.* It means "Gone, gone, completely gone, totally crossed over beyond the farthest shore. So be it."

CHINESE

Chinese is a very different language from Tibetan. It has eight major dialects, none of them mutually intelligible, so that spoken Mandarin is as foreign to a Cantonese speaker as English. But all the Chinese dialects have the same written form, so people can communicate by letter throughout China, and the daily papers are understood by all.

Written Chinese is based on a series of pictograms that once were actual drawings of the things they represent. It is still possible to see, for example, the shape of a man in the character that represents man. Some Chinese characters are very simple, requiring only one or two brush strokes, but others take up to 20 strokes to complete. For children, learning to write this can be very difficult. Each character has to be memorized, unlike in English where a child hearing a new word can make a good guess at its spelling from its pronunciation.

PINYIN

In order to make Chinese intelligible to non-Chinese speakers, a method called pinyin was developed to transliterate Chinese into Roman characters. But pinyin is only a rough transliteration and must be supplemented by a series of stress marks indicating the correct tone. The original phonetic transcription was changed later, causing some problems for foreigners. Using pinyin, Peking becomes Beijing, Mao Tse-tung becomes Mao Zedong, and Canton becomes Guangzhou.

In the 1950s, Chinese characters replaced Tibetan place names. The characters chosen for each place were those that most resembled Tibetan pronunciation. When Tibetan words are then transcribed into pinyin for an English speaker to say, the difference between the original Tibetan sound and the English pronunciation is even greater. For example, one of the monasteries in Tibet is called Tashilhunpo, a literal transcription from the sound of the Tibetan word. But when it is translated through Chinese characters and further transcribed into pinyin it reads Zhaxilhunbo, nothing like the sound of the original word.

Mandarin, the official spoken language of China, has about 400 syllables. Each syllable has four different vocal tones—each tone giving the character a different meaning. For example, the syllable *ma* can mean mother, hemp, horse, or to scold depending on the tone in which it is said.

Getting a job in the civil service or in any industry that involves dealing with the public in Tibet is dependent upon speaking Chinese. In fact, it is becoming more and more usual to hear Tibetans in Lhasa speaking Chinese to one another.

A signpost marking the anniversary of the "Peaceful Liberation" of Tibet. The slogan is written in both Chinese and Tibetan and reads: May all the people of this nation live in unity!

BOOKS AND PRINTING

Books were originally printed in Tibet for the sole purpose of proliferating the Buddhist doctrine. Traditionally, the monasteries produced all printed materials in Tibet. Printing was a very laborious task. First the text was copied on a sheet of paper, then a block of wood was prepared. The page of writing was stuck face down on the block, leaving an impression of the text in reverse on the surface of the block. The paper was then rubbed away and the letters were carved out, a long and tedious process. When the carving was complete, the surface of the carved block was oiled to strengthen it. As copies of the text were needed, the blocks would be taken out, used, and then stored again. Each monastery had large rooms containing thousands of blocks. Only one copy could be made at a time, so individuals were asked to bring their own inks and paper to the monastery.

Traditionally, books were not bound. Each bundle of loose sheets was held together with wooden binding boards, often intricately carved and studded with precious stones, and then wrapped in cloth.

To Tibetans, books are more than just a repository of knowledge. Like mantras, they embody the wisdom or faith or doctrine that they contain. When whole libraries of books were burned and their precious bindings stolen during the Cultural Revolution, it was more than just theft and vandalism to the Tibetans. It was more like desecration.

THE MEDIA

Tibet has two national newspapers, one in Chinese and one in Tibetan. Both are called the *Tibet Daily* and are more or less the same paper with the original Chinese translated into Tibetan.

In every town and city in Tibet there are public address systems that broadcast continuous speeches or instructions, wake people up for work, announce bedtime and times of party meetings. In 1991, the first Tibetan-language radio broadcasts were made by the Voice of America, broadcasting from the Philippines. These were quickly jammed by the Chinese authorities, who then began to produce their own Tibetan-language radio programs.

Television broadcasting began in 1979. The station originally broadcast old Chinese material but now has satellite connections and can transmit live broadcasts from Beijing. There are two channels, one showing dubbed Chinese movies and the other news bulletins and material made in Tibet.

Tibetan movie theaters are often improvised—a sheet is hung on the wall of a community center and movie-goers bring their own stools.

ARTS

THE DEVELOPMENT OF TIBETAN ART FORMS has been motivated and largely influenced by the religion of the country. Painting is confined to mandalas, murals on temple walls, and huge banners called *thangkas* ("THANG-ka") that are hung outside the monasteries during religious festivals. Music is dedicated to prayer chants and hymns. Literature is largely religious in nature, although some much older folk tales have survived from the oral traditions that preceded Buddhism. The grandest architectural forms were reserved for the monasteries and temples, and even craftwork such as jewelry, consisting primarily of amulets or religious symbols, and carpets were religious in nature. Theater is represented by dance drama depicting stories from the Buddhist scriptures.

Opposite: **A fresco painted on the wall of the Jokhang Temple. The wire mesh at the bottom prevents visitors from touching the wall.**

Below: **Pottery making is just one of the many crafts common in Tibet.**

89

This thangka is used for teaching Tibetan medicine at a medical college.

THANGKAS

Thangkas are banners of linen, wool, or silk decorated with special paints. The cloth is stretched out on a frame and spread with a paste made from talcum powder and animal glue; this blocks the pores of the cloth. When the material has dried the outline of the painting is drawn on with charcoal sticks, sometimes from a paper pattern. Painting is done on astrologically favorable days. Often the artist is accompanied by a whole team of laymen and monks whose job it is to make sure that the painting conforms to the rules. When it is completed, a process that can take many years, it is sent to the lama who commissioned it; his hand or footprint is used as a mark of consecration.

Paints are made from minerals such as cinnabar or malachite, or plant dyes mixed with animal glue and ox bile, which gives them a lustre. The finished painting is mounted with a brocade or silk border and rollers at the top and bottom so that it can be displayed. Thangkas are usually rectangular or square and depict Buddhas, deities, pantheons, or the lives of the saints. A very few show the ins and outs of daily life in Tibet. Thangkas are stored in the monastery and hung on the wall during religious festivals.

The hanging of the thangka before a ritual festival is a very important ceremony. Some of them are so big that dozens of monks are required just to haul them out of the store room. Like all Tibetan art, making thangkas is revered as an act of worship.

An elaborately sculpted doorway in the Jokhang Temple.

WOOD CARVING

Wood carving is another example of the dedication and artistry that goes into the decoration of Tibetan temples and shrines. Any part of a temple made of wood is a possible site for wood carvings. Wooden statues of the Buddha and painted wooden tablets with designs similar to the thangkas are also common. Even small shrines in people's houses might be elaborately carved or painted.

SCULPTURE

Stone carvings are a very popular art form in Tibet. The majority of carvings are of a religious nature, such as representations of Buddhist deities, although carved stone lions stand guard at the entrance to many of Tibet's buildings.

Carvings on mountain cliffs or rock faces line the routes that pilgrims take on their way to a monastery or some other religious site. The figures are very simply carved, usually representing the figure of the Buddha or mantras. Pilgrims prostrate themselves before the carvings in the belief that their weariness will be relieved by the act of prayer. Unfortunately, some of these ancient carvings were vandalized during the Cultural Revolution; but many are being painstakingly restored and rebuilt.

A fresco depiction of the wheel of life, an important religious symbol in Tibetan Buddhism.

FRESCOES

These watercolor paintings cover the interior walls of monasteries and temples all over Tibet. Although the Cultural Revolution caused the destruction of these ancient art forms, many of them remain undamaged or at least repairable.

In the 17th century two schools of art developed in Tibet: the Mentang school and the Qenze school. Both schools laid down strict rules about the materials to be used, the proportions of the figures in a fresco, and the nature of the background details. The Buddha figures were to be serene and drawn in single lines with even coloring. The backgrounds were to be painted as if viewed from above, and designs were to be geometric. The brightly colored frescoes depicted a wide range of subjects from scenes of daily working life to religious scenes of the Buddha's lives or images of deities.

BRONZE

Tibetans were mining and sculpting gold, silver, copper, and iron thousands of years ago, using skills adopted from India, Nepal, and China. These influences can be seen in ancient art works as well. Like the monastery frescoes, Buddhist bronzes were governed by strict artistic rules. The exact depiction of a religious statue was described in careful detail so that two images of the same deity would be as nearly identical as possible. Surviving bronzes vary in size from huge statues of the Buddha weighing several tons to tiny ones small enough to be carried on the person.

First the statue was produced in wax and encased in a layer of mud punctured with small holes. This was allowed to harden. The entire model was then heated in an oven until the wax had melted, running out of the holes and leaving the mud mold empty and intact. The mold was then filled with a liquid alloy of copper and tin. When the bronze had cooled sufficiently, the mud walls were broken and the statue was filed to smooth the rough edges. In the case of large statues, the bronze was molded in two halves and then welded together after cooling. The statues were often hollow so they could be filled with precious stones and gold as offerings.

Bronzes like this one are kept in a museum under guard.

LITERATURE

The most important of Tibet's sacred literary works is the 108-volume Kanjur, the translation of the Buddha's words. Similar to the Christian Bible, it is by these words that many Tibetans live their lives. A translation of commentaries on religious ideas and hymns, the Tenjur has 225 volumes. There is also the book known to the West as the Tibetan Book of the Dead, which describes the journey of the soul through the 49 stages of bardo.

Folk literature was mostly preserved in an oral tradition. Storytelling was a family trade and wandering storytellers were in high demand in traditional Tibet. There are many long epic poems such as *Gesar*, the world's longest historic poem, or the songs of Milarepa, a figure famous in Tibetan history.

MILAREPA

Born in 1040 to a family of middle-ranking nobles, Milarepa had every prospect of becoming a wealthy nobleman. But when his father died the estate passed into his uncle's hands until Milarepa came of age. The unscrupulous uncle took the estate for himself and forced Milarepa's mother, brothers, and sisters to become his servants. Milarepa's mother had a tiny piece of property of her own that she sold in order to buy an education in black magic for Milarepa so that he could avenge his family. Milarepa learned well and killed his uncle's eldest son and several others by willing the roof of a house to fall on them. He brought hailstorms to ruin his uncle's crops. When the uncle finally returned Milarepa's property, Milarepa was so overcome by sorrow and guilt at what he had done, he gave up his property and went in search of a holy teacher. He was put to the penance of building and then destroying a tower over and over. Then his teacher taught him to become a monk and to live a life of contemplation. Milarepa lived for many years in a cave where he developed magical powers. Later in life, he wrote some of Tibet's most well-loved poetry and became a saint.

DANCE DRAMA

Tibet has two dance traditions, one dedicated to religion and carried out during religious festivals, and the other a secular tradition performed by traveling groups of laymen. The religious dance dramas were once amazing spectacles that went on for days. They were performed in the courtyards of monasteries by the monks, who often trained for months to get the steps right. The arm movements were based on a form of yoga and legend has it that one performer was able to make rocks explode and once set the Dalai Lama's robe on fire with the power of his performance. Dance dramas were accompanied by music, chanting, and spectacular costumes, including animal masks representing good and evil spirits.

The secular folk operas and plays performed by traveling groups also went on for days. Some were based on famous legends or events from the history of Tibet. Comics were part and parcel of the show and nobody escaped being lampooned, even the lamas. Some of these plays and operas are being revived in modern times.

Many of the traditional dances have been kept alive by communities like the one in Dharmsala where there is no restriction on public performances.

These short-bodied horns are used exclusively for religious music.

MUSIC

Music has always been very important in daily life. There are theme songs for every activity, from important occasions such as weddings to the routines of daily life such as ploughing and begging. Street songs, called *trom gyur shay* ("TROM GIYUR shay"), were popular contemporary songs criticizing local politics or national events.

Religious music uses a very different set of instruments, which have a symbolic nature as well as a function in generating sounds. One such instrument is the thigh-bone trumpet, often made from a human thigh bone and used in a special ceremony called "cutting the go," where an individual attempts to give up all earthly needs and desires in order to reach enlightenment. Another instrument is the double-skull drum made of two skulls with skins stretched over them. An attached bead strikes the two skins as the instrument is flipped from side to side. Conch shells and metal trumpets make a deep booming sound and are often used in religious ceremonies accompanied by the resonating chanting of monks.

POTALA PALACE

The Potala Palace, the home of the Dalai Lamas, is built on an outcrop of rock in Lhasa and dominates the skyline. It is 985 feet (300 meters) long, and contains more than 1,000 rooms. The two palaces inside hold the homes of the Dalai Lamas, seminaries, offices, a printing room, chapels, shrines, and the tombs of the Dalai Lamas. Beneath both palaces lies a vast basement containing storage rooms, libraries, granaries, and a dungeon. It was built over a period of 50 years in the 17th century, commissioned by the Great Fifth Dalai Lama. The Potala was spared from the worst of the desecrations of the Cultural Revolution; its hundreds of chapels and shrines still bear the frescoes and murals and precious artifacts that have been dedicated by pilgrims over the centuries. At the very top of the Potala are two suites of rooms containing relatively modern furniture. These were the living quarters of the last two Dalai Lamas.

ARCHITECTURE

Typical Tibetan city houses are two- or three-story stone buildings with windows overhung by carved wooden eaves. Village houses are built in a rectangle with the outer walls forming a protective barrier and housing an inner courtyard. In Lhasa in particular, the old narrow streets are being replaced with boulevards of office and apartment blocks with tin roofs and wooden partition walls.

The Potala Palace: a masterpiece of architecture.

Tibet's greatest architectural works are its monasteries and temples, which take the form of whole cities built within towering walls. The design of each temple is quite distinct, but many of them are multistory buildings that narrow towards the top. They are often built around a central courtyard and contain prayer halls, libraries, dormitories, printing presses, kitchens, and stables—virtually small cities in themselves. The focal point of every temple is the chorten, a shrine that often holds the remains of some sacred person.

LEISURE

BEFORE 1959, the distinction between religion and other aspects of daily life, such as leisure, was blurred. People spent most of their day in prayer, in the fields or at home, and so in a way religion became the Tibetan's leisure.

Traditionally Tibetans have enjoyed storytelling, gambling, and some sports, although not organized team games. Recently, modern leisure activities such as discos and karaoke have arrived. Reading was primarily a religious activity, as books were revered as sacred objects. This too has changed with the introduction of modern printing methods.

Above: **Watching plays is still a common leisure activity for Tibetans living outside Tibet. It has only been since the 1980s that the Chinese government has relaxed restrictions on cultural events.**

Opposite: **A man and his dog take a moment to relax in the noonday sun.**

Nowadays many Tibetans dedicate their leisure time to rebuilding and refurbishing the many temple complexes damaged during the Cultural Revolution.

Parties were once very popular among the Tibetan nobility, but now there is less leisure time even for the noble families. Despite the lack of time, picnics are still a very popular activity and often last for days.

SPORTS

In the 1940s, sporting activities such as soccer and basketball were unheard of, but now basketball and soccer are played all over Tibet and are almost as widespread as the popular Chinese pastime of table tennis. Tibet has a soccer team that plays in a Chinese league. Billiards has also arrived in Tibet and is played in the open air outside tea shops or beer halls.

Picnicking near the Ganden Monastery. Picnics are a favorite pastime of Tibetans.

Travelers to Tibet in the 1950s described athletic contests between the *dob dobs*. These were small groups of athletic monks who specialized in three competitive sports—running, stone-throwing, and broad jump. They wore loincloths and smeared their faces with soot to make themselves look like formidable opponents. Groups like these, however, were very unusual, and Tibetan monks today generally spend very little time engaged in sports.

PICNICS

Picnics are not just a matter of packing a picnic basket and setting off. The whole business is carefully organized several days ahead of time; it takes a long time to ferry all the necessities out to the picnic site by bicycle. The richer families, or perhaps a work unit, own huge appliquéd tents that they erect. These tents are beautiful works of art decorated with paintings of the wheel of life or other religious symbols. Furniture, rugs, and cushions are brought from the home and placed inside the tents. Food is cooked nearby and served throughout the day while the people lounge around and chat, eat, or play Tibetan board games. As the Tibetan beer begins to flow, storytelling begins as well. The stories can go on for hours and people come and go, hardly paying attention to the plot. Generally the story is a traditional folk tale, like *The Ogress and the Monkey*, forgotten by all but the elderly.

As it gets dark, the dancing begins. Tibetan stamping dances mix with Chinese-style dancing or a version of disco. At night the whole party sleeps under the tent and the next day, when their heads have cleared from the night before, the party continues.

A TRADITIONAL TIBETAN STORY: THE OGRESS AND THE MONKEY

Legend has it that Tibetans' earliest ancestors were a monkey and an ogress whose children were half-human, half-ape. They stood erect, were covered with hair, had flat, red faces, and some say possessed tails. This is the story of their origins and the subsequent evolution of the Tibetan people.

Chenresig, the god of Mercy, and Dolma, his consort, sent their incarnations into Tibet. The incarnation of Chenresig took the form of a monkey. He took vows of celibacy and lived a life of quiet meditation. The incarnation of Dolma was an ogress and a cannibal. She was very lonely and cried and sang sad songs all day long. One day the monkey heard the ogress crying and asked her what was wrong. She told him about her loneliness and begged him to become her husband.

When the monkey went to Chenresig and asked him what he should do, Chenresig told him that he should take the ogress as his wife. They married and had six children. Their children were neither human nor ape, but resembled a cross between the two.

The monkey set aside the southern forests for his children to live in, and there they mated with female monkeys and multiplied. The monkey left his children to survive alone in Tibet, and when he returned they had many descendants—the people of Tibet. They suffered the cold, dry winters and the lack of food, and when the original monkey saw this he was moved by pity for his people. He brought them six kinds of grain—buckwheat, coarse barley, mustard, wheat, rice, and sesame. In this way the first fields were cultivated and the human-apes slowly took on the shape of humans.

The cave where the monkey is said to have lived is now a tourist attraction, and the nearby town is called Zhanang, or playground of the monkeys.

A man showing his children how to play with a toy similar to a yo-yo. There are no Barbie dolls or Leggo sets, so toys are handmade in Tibet.

GAMES

Girim ("gee-RIM") is an ancient game of probable Indian origin that is played all over Tibet. It is similar to billiards with counters dusted in flour being flicked around the board. The object of the game is to get one's counters into one of the four pockets at the corners of the board.

Another popular game is *sho* ("SHO"), a game involving a circle of cowrie shells. Counters are moved around the circle according to the throw of the dice. As the players rattle the dice in the cup, they recite a rhyme asking for the correct number to come up. Games are played ritually at picnics, during festivals, and whenever there is leisure time.

NIGHTLIFE IN LHASA

The Lhasa of old was a garden city full of trees and stone-built houses with intricately carved eaves and balconies. Beggars and domestic animals roamed the streets, and pilgrims walked around the holy places burning juniper wood for offerings.

The Lhasa of today is a new city with a water supply and basic sanitation. Modern hotels, including a brand new Holiday Inn, with all the attendant nightlife of discos, karaoke bars, pool halls, movie theaters, and Chinese and Muslim restaurants, dot the streets of the new city. Meanwhile the old town remains untouched, in defiance of change.

SOCIALIZING

Socializing in some of the smaller towns consists of one or two families turning their living room into a combination bar and restaurant. Tibetans are very friendly and hospitable people and travelers and pilgrims can find shelter and hospitality wherever they go. Among nomad groups, the evening's entertainment takes place wherever they stop for the night and consists of a campfire, lots of Tibetan tea and beer, basic food, and stories.

A center for social life in a town is the tea shop, where groups of friends spend evenings or afternoons. The money is pooled in the center of the table and the tea servers go around refilling the cups with Chinese tea as often as necessary, taking the cost from the pile.

Tea drinking is an important social event in Tibet. Tibetan tea is a meal in itself, full of barley flour and butter and whatever else is considered necessary for the occasion. Visitors are always offered tea when they visit a home and it is impolite not to accept it. Custom dictates that as long as the visit lasts, the cup should be refilled.

A common way to unwind in Tibet is to meet for a few drinks after a hard day's work.

FESTIVALS

THERE ARE MANY FESTIVALS in the Tibetan calendar, most of them religious in nature. These festivals would once have been national celebrations, with all the people of Tibet flocking to the nearest large town to witness the events. Nomads would bring in things for trade and the streets would fill up with pilgrims. For 20 years or so, all of this has disappeared, but the recent new freedom means that some Tibetans are now witnessing some ancient festivals for the first time. The rites are only understood by a few old men.

THE TIBETAN CALENDAR

The Tibetan calendar is based on the phases of the moon rather than the sun. Because of this, the Tibetan year begins sometime in February just as the Chinese year does. Since lunar phases do not occur every 30 days, additional days are included in the calendar at auspicious times to coordinate the seasons and the months. Tibet's calendar has 12 months, but some of these may not actually take place if the stars suggest that the month may be a bad one. One tourist staying in Tibet reported that the month equivalent to July was abandoned and instead there were two Augusts.

The Tibetan calendar begins with the birth of the Buddha and works in 60-year cycles. Each cycle is named after one of the mystical elements—fire, earth, iron, water, or wood. The first half of the cycle is represented by the name and characteristics of a male animal, the second by those of a female animal—for example, 1940 was the year of the Iron Dragon.

Opposite: **A Tibetan monk dancer performs a ritual dance for an audience in Darjeeling, India.**

Below: **When historians began to study Tibetan history, they were obliged to learn the Tibetan calendar system in order to determine the exact dates of events.**

THE NEW YEAR FESTIVAL

New Year's preparations are long and arduous in order to prevent demons like this one from affecting life in the coming year.

Using the Tibetan lunar calendar, New Year celebrations begin on the last day of the 12th lunar month. Before the day arrives, people begin to prepare by cleaning their houses, washing themselves and their clothes, and buying new material to make quilt covers and clothes. In the kitchen, the women busy themselves making special New Year pastries called *khabtse* ("CAB-tse"), which are left as offerings at the temple and given to visitors.

The house is decorated with the eight auspicious signs, which include conch shells (signifying the Buddha's enlightenment), dharma wheels, and eternal knots (signifying love and harmony). A swastika, the symbol of luck, is painted on the front door, and the ceiling beams are painted with white dots to bring long life and good harvests.

On the last night of the year, the house is swept clean and the dust piled into a corner. On top of the pile of dust are placed tiny models of evil spirits made out of dough. When the women have rebraided their hair and everyone has dressed in

new clothes, the family sits down to the last meal of the year. A soup called *guthuk* ("GUH-thuk") is prepared especially for the occasion.

After the meal, the eldest member of the family rubs a ball of dough over each family member to draw out all the illnesses they have suffered over the year. Following this, the whole family collects a pile of dust, which is carried across the road and thrown on a communal fire. The sweeping of the dust symbolizes the family's ridding the house of demons. When the dust is thrown on the fire, the demons burn while the family shout and set off fireworks to scare them back to their world.

In the time of the Dalai Lama, there were ritual dances, horse races, and archery competitions to bring in the New Year. Some of these traditions are beginning to reemerge, most notably an annual horseback riding tournament. In the competition, horsemen ride towards a target and try to hit it first with a bow and arrow and then with a musket.

Men prepare to mount their horses to take part in the equestrian competition.

A crowd of people gathers for the New Year's Day celebrations.

NEW YEAR'S DAY

All Tibetans get up very early on New Year's day and dress in their best clothes. (For many years, everyone had to wear green or grey work clothes, but recently more people are wearing national dress.) People visit each other's houses and at each house are offered wheat and tsampa from an offering box. New prayer flags are printed on brightly colored cloth according to the elements of the birth years of the family and are hung out in streams from the rooftops. The family link hands and walk around the flat roof of their house, throwing handfuls of beer and barley dough as an offering and calling *La le go ("la LE go"),* "Victory to the gods."

Once the friendly exchanges have been made, families make their way to the Potala. Pilgrims climb the hundreds of steps to the top of the palace, turning prayer wheels as they go and repeating mantras to help them concentrate on their prayers. When particular statues or sacred objects are passed, the pilgrims prostrate themselves on the ground in reverence.

MONLAM

The New Year festival called Monlam goes on for 15 days. In Lhasa, the Potala is the center of the ceremonies of prayer, tea drinking, and singing. Student-monks sitting for the rank of *geshe* ("GE-shay") debate with their seniors, pilgrims bring huge sacks of offerings to the temple, and travelers sleep in the streets of Lhasa, lighting fires to keep warm.

The 15th day is the butter festival. It is said to have originated when the fifth Dalai Lama had a dream of paradise and wishing to show his followers what it looked like, modeled it in butter. In the past, every noble family made a sculpture out of butter and donated it to the temple. Now this duty is performed by the monks using butter colored with dye. Huge dragons and lotus flowers and mythological figures surround images of the Buddha, all of them carved out of Tibetan butter (the consistency is similar to that of cheese). Pilgrims circle the sculptures repeating their prayers all night long. As the sun rises, the butter sculptures begin to melt, illustrating the Buddhist belief in the transient nature of everything.

The Monlam festival ends with the parading of the statue of Jampa, the future Buddha, around the main square in Lhasa accompanied by the sound of a Tibetan orchestra. Pilgrims cover the statue in silk scarves as a sign of respect before the statue is returned to the temple.

Sculptures like this one, constructed entirely of butter, are commonly made during the Monlam festival and given to the temples as offerings.

Monks leading a procession from the Potala Palace through the streets of Lhasa.

THE GOLDEN STAR FESTIVAL

For the monks, the months leading up to the Golden Star Festival are spent inside the monasteries to avoid killing any newly born insects whose incarnation might be prematurely ended by being stepped on. The Golden Star Festival, or Sho Dun, marks the end of a long period celebrating the washing away of passion, greed, and jealousy. The monks come down from the temple to be treated to drama and opera by the people of the city. In the past, these operas and plays would have been performed by groups of amateur actors from all over Tibet who performed the plays as part of their village's taxation. These days, performances by state-run dance and drama groups are staged. The monks are given yogurt as part of the banquet prepared for them. Families and work units arrange three or four day picnics in the parks surrounding the Potala Palace, sleeping under beautiful canopies, eating, and playing games. The festival is also marked by ritual bathing and the ritual washing of clothes in the river.

OTHER FESTIVALS

The festival called *Chokor Duchen* ("CHOK-or DUTCH-en") on the fourth day of the sixth lunar month marks the Buddha's first sermon. On this day monasteries display huge thangkas on the monastery walls, and the day is spent in prayer. Some pilgrims spend the day climbing Tibet's holy mountains.

The Festival of the Lamps on the 25th day of the 10th lunar month commemorates the death of Tsongkapa, the founder of the Yellow Hat school of Buddhism. Fires are lit on the roofs of the monasteries and people light lamps and butter candles in his memory.

The Scapegoat Festival, which takes place on the 28th day of the second lunar month, is a spectacular event accompanied by ritual acts in dance drama. The festival begins as the monks form a procession wearing black robes. This is followed by troupes of dancers dressed in costumes and wearing huge masks depicting demons, who whirl and shriek to the sound of discordant music. Dancers dressed as the saints chase away the demons and perform a more stately and dignified dance. A figure made of dough and filled with colored inner organs is torn to pieces. It is the scapegoat representing all the evils of the world.

These performances once went on for many days in the temples and monasteries of Tibet, but many of them have not yet been revived, and those that have are often more sober occasions than they would have been years ago.

Robed and masked dancers perform a dance drama for an appreciative crowd in northern India.

FOOD

DURING THE 1960s and 1970s, Tibet experienced severe food shortages as the Chinese authorities tried to impose a system of communal farming all across China. Farmers had to plant wheat instead of the hardier barley, which is better suited to Tibet's climate. The thin, underfertilized soil was unable to support the intensive farming methods introduced by the Chinese. The situation became very grave.

Today, besides the communes, people are allowed to own their own yaks again and the nomads are back on the northern plain moving with their animals. Barley has replaced wheat once more, and a greater variety of food has come to Tibet in the form of canned or fresh imported food from the rest of China.

YAK PRODUCTS

The great staple of the Tibetan diet is the yak. This sturdy creature, a little like a cross between a cow and a buffalo, has provided the basic necessities of life for Tibetan people for thousands of years. On the Northern Plateau, the yak is the only form of food available because vegetables do not grow in the dry, cold climate. In the southern part of the country, yak meat is often supplemented by vegetables, nuts and fruit, and the second staple—barley.

Yaks provide much more than just food for the Tibetans. The hide is used to make clothes, bags, shoes, and houses. Even the bones are used as utensils and jewelry. Besides all this are the many food items produced from yaks. The female produces milk with a very high fat content. Unlike people in other countries, Tibetans do

Opposite: **Mother and child enjoying a hot bowl of soup on a cold day.**

Below: **Dried yak dung is stacked outside the kitchen and used as fuel for the cooking fire.**

Butter wrapped in yak skin and sold in the Lhasa market. Tibetan yak butter is closer to the consistency of cheese than of butter.

not worry about high cholesterol levels; fat is an essential part of the diet in Tibet. The low temperatures and the high degree of manual work demand high calorie consumption, making yak milk an invaluable food item.

BUTTER Yak milk is used primarily to make butter. The milk is emptied into a butter churn, an essential part of Tibetan kitchen equipment, where it is stirred, or churned, until it begins to thicken. Once the milk solidifies, it is wrapped in skins and taken to the market to be sold or stored sealed in the skins for long periods. When the skins are opened, the butter begins to decay, producing veins of mold similar to blue cheese. But this process is much slower than it is in most cheese-producing countries because the cold, dry weather does not encourage decay.

YOGURT Another favorite use for yak milk is to make yogurt. This is a rare delicacy now in the southern part of Tibet but can still be bought in the markets for a price. The test of a good yogurt is to turn it upside down. If the yogurt does not fall out of the jar it is good and fresh. During the summer yogurt plays an important part in the Golden Star Festival, when it is served to the monks who have been cloistered away in their monasteries for several weeks.

To make yogurt, the yak milk collected at the evening milking is boiled and left to settle with a tiny piece of yogurt from the last batch. The live bacteria in the sample acts on the fresh milk and turns it overnight into fresh yogurt. Some of this is in turn added to the next batch in the morning. Sometimes sugar is added to sweeten the yogurt if it is available, but sugar is an expensive import.

CHEESE After butter, the most important use for yak milk is to make cheese. Initially, the milk is boiled and poured into a mold. A setting agent is added to ensure that the milk will solidify. Once the cheese grows a hard outer shell, it

Men bartering over yak meat in the market. According to Buddhist tradition, it is a sin to slaughter an animal, but it is perfectly acceptable to buy butchered meat.

is stored away for many months. When the cheese is ready for consumption, it is cut into cubes, strung together like a necklace, and worn around the neck ready to eat. A cube of this kind of cheese is very hard but very nutritious and sweeter than what one might expect of cheese. It can take up to an hour of turning around in the mouth before it is soft enough to swallow.

YAK MEAT Similar to beef except slightly stronger in taste, yak meat is becoming a tourist favorite. In countries like Nepal, it is now possible to order a yak steak or a yak burger. But typical Tibetan yak meat cuisine is raw dried meat. In a country where freezers and electricity are a luxury, the best means of preserving the goodness of the meat is to hang it up in the dry, germ-free Tibetan air. As the meat is needed, it is sliced off the carcass and either gnawed raw or added to a thick, gruel-like stew.

Despite the fact that there is plentiful wildlife on the Northern Plateau, the nomads never hunt for their food.

FOOD TABOOS

Goats, sheep, and chickens are bred, but they are less popular than yaks because they are small and necessitate more slaughter. The slaughter of animals and the fresh meat industry is handled by Tibet's Muslims, who butcher the animals according to Muslim custom. Occupations such as these are abhorred by Tibetan Buddhists, whose religious ethics forbid them from killing unnecessarily. If the slaughter of an animal is necessary for the survival of the family, the Tibetan Buddhist will say a quick prayer over the animal before killing it.

Because of Tibetan funeral customs, people are forbidden to catch fish for food. Although less common than other burial methods, the bodies of the dead are sometimes thrown into the river to be consumed by the fish as a gesture of giving back what one has taken from this world. Eating the fish that would have consumed the bodies is objectionable to Tibetan Buddhists. For the Chinese, however, fish is a delicacy and a common ingredient in Chinese cooking.

A family in Lhasa eating breakfast.

GRAINS AND VEGETABLES

The staple food of most Tibetans is barley flour. Barley is a hardy plant that can survive in poor soil and dry conditions, so it is widely grown in Tibet. The harvested barley grains are roasted in small quantities in hot sand over a stove and then ground. The flour has a nutty taste, and when mixed with Tibetan tea, becomes a meal in itself, called tsampa. The bowl is turned with the left hand while the right hand kneads the dough into a soft ball. The ball is then eaten like a soft donut. Yogurt,

116

Cabbage is one of the only vegetables that grows summer and winter despite frost, snow, and wind.

sugar, or raisins can be added to give a sweet flavor. Because the flour has been roasted it does not taste raw. Outside of the major cities, tsampa is often the only food available.

Wheat, although grown in Tibet, is less hardy than barley and is more of a luxury item. It is used to make unleavened bread and to make a fine thin pastry covering for small pies and cakes and to make noodles. Rarer still are grains such as buckwheat and corn, which form a part of the diet in some regions. They are both ground into flour and roasted or baked as bread.

In many parts of Tibet green vegetables are a rarity and are only available as imported canned goods. In the south, green vegetables such as cabbage are grown and some wild plants are gathered for food, especially nettles, which are often a large part of the diet of hermit monks. Herbs too are gathered from the wild both for medicine and to flavor food. Chilies are an important flavoring in Tibetan food and are also eaten as snacks—like fresh chili smeared in lard.

Fruits such as pears, apples, peaches, and tangerines grow in Tibet. In the cities these are available dried, as are figs, raisins, dried persimmons, cashew nuts, and peanuts.

SOME TIBETAN DISHES

Everyone carries with them their store of ground barley flour, a string of cheese cubes, perhaps a precious supply of sugar, the ingredients for tea, and a wooden bowl. All that is needed to make a typical Tibetan meal is some hot water, butter, and salt.

A more complicated evening meal might be made from wheat flour noodles cooked in boiling water with some onion, chili, and pieces of meat added. Eggs are often eaten hard-boiled or as an omelet with vegetables and chili.

A special dish eaten on the eve of the New Year is a thick stew called *guthuk* made from meat and vegetables and thickened with barley flour. Another festive delicacy is called *momos* ("MOH-mohs"). These are dumplings made from thin sheets of wheat flour wrapped around spiced meat and steamed.

The few restaurants that have opened to cater to tourists usually serve Chinese Sichuan dishes. These include stir-fried pieces of meat and vegetables cooked very quickly with lots of chilies.

TIBETAN TEA

Tibetan tea is by all accounts an acquired taste. It is made from tea leaves, butter, salt, and barley flour. First, the tea is boiled in a huge pot with wood ash soda (added to bring out the color) until the dried leaves have infused. The tea is strained into a large wooden pot like a butter churn and melted butter and salt are added. A plunger is inserted and pumped to emulsify the butter, and finally barley flour is added before the whole mixture is churned.

The result is a thin, savoury soup. Most people drink between 60 and 80 cups of this tea a day. It provides the bulk of their calories. When the tea is first poured into the drinking bowls a scum of butter floats to the top. This is skimmed off and kept either for animal fodder or among the very poor is recycled into the next brew. The tea maker makes gallons of tea at a time and it is kept always ready. Visitors are always offered tea, and it is impolite to refuse.

These nomads have established a grassland market and restaurant for weary travelers to have a cup of tea and buy supplies.

OTHER DRINKS

In bigger towns, tea shops sell Chinese tea sweetened with imported sugar and milk. The main alcoholic drink is *chang*—home-made beer brewed from fermented barley. It has a sour taste and low alcohol content. The same mixture is often distilled into a spirit called *arak* ("a-RACK"), which is much more potent. There are also many imported alcoholic drinks in the bars of Lhasa, especially the Chinese beer called Tsingtao, as well as Chinese versions of cola and carbonated fruit drinks.

Serving up chang.

A TIBETAN FEAST

Heinrich Harrer and other travelers to Tibet during the 1940s and 1950s have described a typical Tibetan feast as a day-long affair beginning with Chinese-style tea and cakes in the morning at about 11 a.m. and followed by Chinese-style lunch at about midday. Vegetables covered in spicy sauce, shark's fin soup, noodles, and rice were the most common dishes. The afternoon brought more cakes and tea, and the evening meal would be the most splendid, starting off with things to nibble: cashew nuts, pumpkin seeds, and pickled fruit. This was followed by yak or mutton cooked in several different ways, then by rice and sweets. Chang, orange juice, and tea would accompany the meal.

A modern visitor to Tibet describes a more modest Tibetan dinner party as consisting of chunks of dried yak meat, tsampa cake made with sugar (shown cooking below), cheese, and chang.

Wood is a rare commodity in Tibet and is rarely used for a cooking fire. The main fuel is dried yak dung.

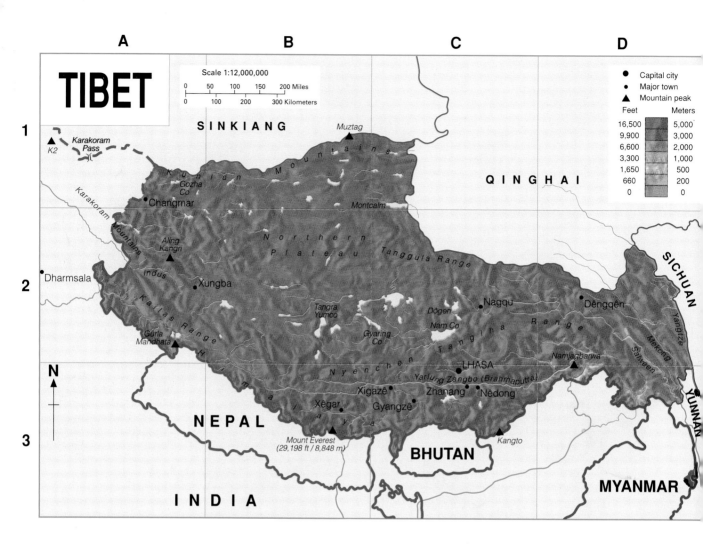

TIBET

Scale 1:12,000,000

0   50   100   150   200 Miles
0   100   200   300 Kilometers

- ● Capital city
- ● Major town
- ▲ Mountain peak

Feet	Meters
16,500	5,000
9,900	3,000
6,600	2,000
3,300	1,000
1,650	500
660	200
0	0

A   B   C   D

1

SINKIANG

Muztag

QINGHAI

K2

Karakoram
Pass

Kunlun   Mountains

Gozha
Co

Changmar

Montcalm

2

Dharmsala

Aling
Kangri

Northern

Plateau

Tanggula Range

SICHUAN

Indus

Xungba

Nagqu

Dêngqên

Yangtze

Kailas Range

Tangra
Yumco

Dogen

Tanggula   Range

Mekong

Salween

Gürla
Mandhata

Gyaring
Co

Nam Co

Namjagbarwa

N

Nyenchen

LHASA

Xigazê

Yarlung Zangbo (Brahmaputra)

Zhanang

Nêdong

YUNNAN

3

Xêgar

Gyangzê

NEPAL

Mount Everest
(29,198 ft / 8,848 m)

BHUTAN

Kangto

MYANMAR

INDIA

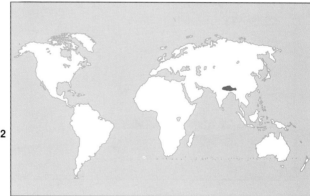

QUICK NOTES

LAND AREA
474,008 square miles (1,228,000 square kilometers)

POPULATION
2,280,000 (1992)

POPULATION DENSITY
4.7 people per square mile (1.8 people per square kilometer)

CAPITAL
Lhasa

OTHER MAJOR TOWNS
Xigazê, Gyangzê, Zhanang, Nêdong

HIGHEST MOUNTAINS
Everest - 29,198 feet (8,848m)
Namjagbarwa - 25,445 feet (7,756 m)
Gurla Mandhata - 25,355 feet (7,728 m)

MAJOR RIVERS
The Indus, Brahmaputra, Ganges, Sutlej, Mekong, and Yangtze rivers all have their headwaters in Tibet

CLIMATE
Semi-arid

AVERAGE RAINFALL
15 inches (38.1 cm) per year

AVERAGE ANNUAL TEMPERATURE
34° F (1.1 ° C)

MAIN EXPORT
Timber

MAIN IMPORTS
Manufactured goods, rice, Chinese tea, and sugar

FORM OF GOVERNMENT
Autonomous Province of the People's Republic of China administered by the Tibetan Communist Party Committee

LANGUAGES
Tibetan, Chinese

CURRENCY
Remimbi (One yuan = 30 US cents)

MAIN RELIGION
Tibetan Buddhism

IMPORTANT ANNIVERSARIES
New Year festival, first to seventh day of first month
Monlam festival, fourth to fifth day of the first month
Birth of Buddha Sakyamuni, seventh day of the fourth month
Buddha Sakyamuni's first sermon, fourth day of the sixth month

RELIGIOUS LEADERS
Dalai Lama, Panchen Lama

GLOSSARY

Bhotia
A group of people who are ethnically Tibetan but live within the borders of India.

Bön
The earliest known form of religion in Tibet.

chuba ("CHOO-pa")
An overcoat, often made of sheepskin, traditionally worn in Himalayan countries.

chang
A nourishing Tibetan drink made from barley, similar to beer.

dob dobs ("DOB dobs")
Small groups of monks who took part in competitions to test their athletic prowess.

dzo ("ZO")
A cross between a yak and a cow.

Gelukpa
The Yellow Hat Buddhist sect, which ruled Tibet politically and spiritually before the invasion of the Chinese. Its spiritual head is the Dalai Lama.

geshe ("GE-shay")
A monk who has passed the initial stages of progress towards lamahood.

girim ("gee-RIM")
An ancient Indian game played all over Tibet.

guthuk ("GUH-thuk")
A thick soup-stew eaten at New Year's.

Lamaism
The name given to Tibetan Buddhism, which depends heavily on spiritual guidance from a spiritual leader called a lama.

mandalas
A complex geometric pattern representing some aspect of Buddhist religion.

mantra
A sacred formula repeated as an incantation in meditation.

pinyin
The system for representing the sound of a Chinese word in Roman characters.

sho ("SHO")
A popular Tibetan game in which rhymes are recited when the dice are thrown.

thangkas ("THANG-kas")
Banners hung on the monastery walls during religious festivals.

tsampa ("tsam-PA")
Tibetan bread made from barley flour, tea, and butter.

tsha tsha ("CHA cha")
A small medallion made of clay worn as an amulet.

BIBLIOGRAPHY

Dalai Lama. *The Autobiography of His Holiness the Dalai Lama, My Land, My People.* Edited by David Howarth. London: Weidenfeld and Nicholson, 1962.

Gibb, Christopher. *The Dalai Lama: the Exiled Leader of the People of Tibet and Tireless Worker for World Peace.* Milwaukee: Gareth Stevens Children's Books, 1990.

Goldstein, Melvyn C. *Nomads of Western Tibet: The Survival of a Way of Life.* Berkeley: University of California Press, 1990.

Kalman, Bobbie. *Tibet.* Toronto: Crabtree Publishing Co., 1989.

Kendra, Judith. *Tibetans.* New York: Thomson Learning, 1994.

Normanton, Simon. *Tibet: The Lost Civilisation.* New York: Viking Penguin Inc., 1989.

Reynolds, Jim. *The Outer Path: Finding My Way in Tibet.* Sunnyvale: Fair Oaks Publications, 1992.

INDEX

INDEX

INDEX

PICTURE CREDITS

Richard L'Anson: 1, 6, 11, 14, 33, 37, 41, 42, 44, 49, 55, 58, 68, 78, 97, 103
Camera Press: 30, 76
Focus Team: 16, 57
Mark de Fraeye: 4, 20, 21, 34, 38, 39, 67, 81, 83, 86, 88, 92, 93, 106, 112, 113, back cover
HBL Network: 51, 54, 82, 95
Hulton-Deutsch: 24. 26, 109
Hutchison Library: 13, 18, 28, 35, 62, 65 (above), 65 (below), 69, 73, 80, 85, 89, 91, 96, 114, 116, 119
Image Bank: front cover, 10, 15, 48, 100, 108
Life File: 22, 27, 29, 40, 45, 61, 90, 110, 121
Björn Klingwall: 8, 52, 53, 58, 63, 71, 79, 102, 107, 115, 118, 120
Photo Bank: 4, 74, 75, 98, 105
Travel Ink: 47
Veronique Sanson: 3, 25, 31, 46, 77, 99, 104, 111